WRITE~~PUBLISH~~MARKET

A step-by-step for each phase

Ann Everett

TABLE OF CONTENTS

Write~Publish~Market

WRITE

Introduction

Before I get to the stages, I want to talk about having a plan in place. The more books you have published, the better chance you have of being successful. And by successful, I don't mean becoming a NYT or USA bestseller. If you achieve that, then congratulations! However, you can enjoy a profitable business without reaching that status.

Series, trilogies and companion books are popular today because continuing stories SELL. Once your readers get invested in your characters, they want more. Another popular trend is series novellas. The advantage to doing any of these things is the ability to cross promote.

Also, by including teasers in the back of each book guiding your reader to the rest of the series, is perpetual marketing!

When my first book, *Laid Out and Candle Lit*, was published, I knew it would be the first in a series of three, set in the same location, with the same main characters, yet stand-alone stories. In those books, I have Sweet Thangs Bakery, where many scenes take place. Part of my plan was to publish a cookbook based on the fictional business. It took three years to complete, but finally, *Sweet Thangs, Southern Sweets from Two Sassy Sisters*, came out in 2014.

Since it is a non-fiction book, it opens other avenues of marketing for my novels. When I promote it, I also promote the trilogy and vice versa. This is something you should consider. Does one of your characters give advice? Design or decorate houses? Do you have one who is a weapons expert? Or owns a catering business? Maybe you have a character involved in the fashion world. If you do, all those things can lead to either a non-fiction book about their expertise OR a successful blog.

With my romance novels, I didn't plan on writing companion stories, but in *Tell Me a Secret* and *Two Wrongs Make a Right*, each book had a secondary character readers loved. Jared, from *Tell Me a Secret*, and Raynie, from *Two Wrongs Make a Right*. When that happened, I thought why not give those two their own story—which led to *Say You'll Never Love Me*. By doing so, it connected all three books. Sometimes, your readers show you the way!!

So, before you get started, do some brainstorming. Adding likable characters who don't take center stage, but steal scenes with witty dialogue or quirky actions, gives you the opportunity to write another story!

Consider these:

Continuing sagas

Spin-offs of secondary characters

Standalone novels with the same characters

A new story set in the same location, universe or world

Later generational stories

SIX STAGES OF WRITING

IDEA

You've come up with an idea for a book—or maybe you want to try your hand at writing—and need an idea. If that's the case, there are sites where you can find plots.

This site offers ideas, tips, and courses. If you subscribe to their newsletter, you'll get a free eBook of 30 Inspirational Ideas.
http://www.creative-writing-now.com/story-starters.html

Find writing prompts along with a ton of other useful information on this site.
http://www.writersdigest.com/prompts

A list of over 2,000 scenarios to ignite your imagination.
http://www.angelfire.com/nc/tcrpress/plotbank.html

OR, you can do it by listening in on conversations while you're in line at the grocery store, or in a doctor's office waiting room. Maybe an article in a newspaper or magazine sparked an idea and got you to thinking—hmm?

Once you have the idea, you can either outline, which makes you a planner, or dive right in and put fingers to keyboard, which makes you a pantster.

I've done both and planning works better, and writing goes smoother. However, sometimes I have no idea where the story is going beyond the first few chapters, so outlining isn't possible. Once I'm into the story and get a vision for it, I'll make a loose outline. Then, as I think of more scenes, even dialogue I want to use, I'll add those to my notes.

I use a dry-erase board. That makes it easy for me to move things around, or make adjustments.

I'm old school, but you may want to use a tool that allows you to write your first draft in a program with the ability to control formatting and convert documents into other types of files. If so, I recommend Scrivener. There is a learning curve, but authors who use it, swear by it. As of this printing, the cost of the program is about $40. Here's the purchase site.
https://www.literatureandlatte.com/scrivener.php

RESEARCH

Once you have an idea, then you'll need to do some research to find out if your brilliant plan is feasible. If so, here are some sources to help.

Ask questions about pretty much anything and find an answer.
http://www.chacha.com

Thousands of topics from engines to lock-picking to ESP, with videos and illustrations, are explained here.
http://www.howstuffworks.com/

Send Dr. Lyle a question following his guidelines, and he'll answer, many times within the same day.
http://www.dplylemd.com

Even though you're writing fiction, you need to have your facts right.

Mention a full moon on a certain date? There had better be a full moon on that date!

Write something about an animal, then make sure you're right.

Is your book set in a past era? Watch your language. Don't have your characters using modern words not used in that time period.

Do you describe certain flowers growing in a field or along a highway? Make sure that particular flower grows in that region and at that time of year.

I mention these things because readers will call you out on them! More importantly, the mistake will stop your reader and take them out of your story. You don't want that to happen. If you have too many facts wrong, you'll lose credibility. If the reader decides you don't know what you're writing about, they may put your book down, never to pick it up again.

In addition to researching plot ideas and verifying facts, the internet is flooded with generators to help you with names and descriptions of your characters—even book titles!

This site will generate names for fictional locations, character names and profiles, first lines, and plot twists. They also have a "fun" section that suggests ex-lover insults, and pet names for lovers. It is a UK site, so the names are British, but with a little work, you can adapt them to anywhere.
http://writers-den.pantomimepony.co.uk/writers-locations.php

The location generator button gave me these:

Deedfield-a small town.

Dreworth-a leafy suburb that was once on an ancient trade route.

Houburn House-the newly built villa of a successful businessman on its own private estate.

Name generator produced these:

Male name-Daryl Callcut

Female name-Antonia Callcut

Male name-Orsino Rossi

Female name-Fabiana Rossi

Here is another site with tons of generators. Characters, combat, darkness, evil, magic, humor, skills, abilities, and traits are just a few. Even if you use nothing from these sites, they are a lot of fun!
http://www.seventhsanctum.com/index-writ.php

Here are a few examples of some I mentioned and what they generated.

Character

This man makes you think of a playful puppy. He has narrow brown eyes like two discs of wood. His luxurious, straight, bone-white hair is worn in a style that reminds you of a gush of water. He has a broad-shouldered build. His skin is pale. He has a high forehead and thin lips. His wardrobe is strange.

Combat

(Wrestling moves) Argentine Gutwrench, Open Leg Fist, Ring Rope Slam, Turnbuckle Death Takedown.

Darkness/evil

(Rituals) Ancestral Enchantment of the Bone of Limbo, Conjuration of Demigods, Dark Wraiths' Sacrament of Fear.

Magic

(Potions) The bubbling tonic is cerulean in color. It smells and tastes like milk and garlic—the fizzing, opalescent elixir is black in color. It smells and tastes like licorice—the frothing, viscous draught is arisen with cerulean flecks. It smells like chemicals but tastes like salt.

Western and Old West Names

http://www.mithrilandmages.com/utilities/Western.php

Female:
*Amma Lila Pelen
Altha Glennie Search
Veronica Alwina Flock
Emelia Nola Bombarger
Courtney Vina Albert*

Male:

Ewin Milt McGiven
Fuller Clell Retzman
Elsberry Allie Fox
Carol Reason Rosenauer
Anatole Benjamen McMurphy

On this same site, you can also find names for cities, businesses, restaurants, ships/boats, streets, medieval and modern names.

To find a generator for your needs, search your subject. Example: Romance book title generator, Fantasy name generator, etc. You'll find numerous sites! Heck, you can even find a site that will convert your name into a stripper moniker!! If you try it, be prepared for some risqué results!!

One of the best ways to find a resource is by attending conferences or venues where you interact with other authors who may have experience in an area you need. Several years ago at a local writer's workshop, I sat with a fellow writer during lunch who happened to be a police detective. I mentioned I might have questions concerning police procedure from time to time, and he volunteered to help. He turned out to be a fantastic source!

ROUGH DRAFT

A rough draft sometimes referred to as a first draft, is just that. It's meant to get words on the page. Get your basic story written and not worry about the technical aspect. You want to write it the best you can, but don't get bogged down with things like comma placement, repeat words, description, introspection, etc. Those can be corrected and added in re-writing. If you stop to correct mistakes during first/rough drafts, you may never get the story written!

This is the time to concentrate on plot, development of characters, setting, and the beginning of your story arc. This is where you'll establish the purpose of your heroine and hero. What problems or challenges they face. What needs to happen to solve those things? What stands in the way of reaching the solutions?

There is a cycle of fiction writing. Narrative. Action. Dialogue. Repeat. You don't have to use them in the order I have listed, but you do have to balance the three. You should include description in all of those elements. Any successful writer will have those components repeated throughout their story. Too much of one or the other and the story becomes tedious.

If you're writing in third person, choose point of view by determining who has the most to lose or gain in each scene. Which character will change the most? Maybe your hero is a scoundrel in the first few chapters but transforms as the story progresses. Perhaps your heroine has a major hurdle she needs to overcome, and if so, that change needs to happen in small steps to build tension and move your story arc forward to a rewarding resolution.

Remember, your rough/first draft is the bare bones of your story. You can flesh out your characters, breathe life into your settings, add sensory elements, correct errors, and mistakes in the next draft.

That's how I write. It may not work for you. You may be the type who must make each chapter as perfect in every way as you write. If that's your method, then go with it. You know what works best for you.

I don't remember who said to write one page a day for a whole year, and you'd have a book! True, and that's great if a daily schedule fits your life, but if not, then write when you can and don't put yourself under pressure. The same routine doesn't work for everyone.

But keep in mind, writing, like any other job, demands discipline and the longer you're away from it, the harder it is to get back into the habit.

According to some, action in your dreams takes the same amount of time as if you were performing the feat. So if you're dreaming of mixing a cake, and it takes you 15 minutes to do in real time, then the dream will last 15 minutes. I'm not sure that's true. However, in fiction writing, it is a good idea to know exactly how long something will take or what will happen to the character while he carries out the action.

If you have a character exploring an abandoned house, you may not be able to describe what he sees, hears, and smells, unless you experience the same thing.

Maybe you have a coffee shop or grocery store scene. What about a hair salon or mechanic's garage? You'll be able to write a more realistic description if you experience those places first hand. Visit similar places and make notes.

CRITIQUE

Why is it we can't find any fault in our own writing but have no trouble spotting errors and mistakes in someone else's? In my humble opinion, it is necessary to get critique. I belong to a local group where I read chapters aloud, and members offer suggestions for improvement.

Not only do I get help with my story, but by giving critique and listening to others critique, I hone my skills.

I also belong to an online group with a broad cross-section of readers, in location, age, and expertise. Some reviewers are good with punctuation. Some with grammar. Others with logic, pace, plot, action, POV, etc. An outside perspective of 'fresh eyes' helps polish your prose. If you don't live in an area with writing/critique groups, you can find plenty just a few short keystrokes away.

There are numerous sites to choose from, offering free services and paid memberships. Let's talk about the paid sites first. Most work the same way. For a small monthly charge, you read and critique chapters of other writers to gain points, then use those points to post your work and receive critique.

If readers like your story, they'll read from beginning to end, become familiar with your voice, and get to know your characters. They'll point out problem areas not only with the technical side of writing but also plot, pace, dialogue, etc.

All critique partners won't be a perfect match. They may be a nice person, but just not right for you. If that happens, thank them for their review, and most of the time if you don't reciprocate by reading their work, they won't review you again.

Below, I've listed two sites that require membership. They accept most genres. I've belonged to The Next Big Writer for several years and recommend it.

http://www.thenextbigwriter.com
http://www.fanstory.com

The following list is for free sites. Check each one for how they operate. Some match you with a partner or require a certain amount of critiques each month, while others must 'approve' your membership.

http://www.ladieswhocritique.com
http://www.critiquecircle.com
http://www.critique.org/workshops
http://www.mysterywritersforum.com
http://www.scribophile.com

You can also find critique partners on Facebook and Goodreads by searching "critique groups" in your genre.

REWRITING

Some think rewriting is another form of editing. Not me. Rewriting gives me the opportunity to flesh out my scenes and add introspection. I skimp on those things in first drafts. At this point, I'm still not editing, which means I'm not trying to get the punctuation correct or any of the other technical stuff. I'm just trying to make the story better. Get into deep POV of my characters. Make the scenes more descriptive. Work on transitioning smoothly from one scene to the next. Concentrate on sentence starts and weed out pronoun and proper noun beginnings.

I also have a bad habit in first drafts of using time as a transition—an hour later—fifteen minutes later, etc. This is the point where I try to replace those.

I don't wait until I've finished the book to rewrite. Well, I do rewrite after I've finished it, but I also rewrote as the chapters were critiqued. If a reader offers me comma help, I put it in because I can't place commas correctly to save my soul! If they suggest improvement for a scene, I may not change it then, but I make a note in red at the point that needs attention.

You can do revision whenever you like. As you go along, or when the book is finished.

Rewriting is my favorite part of the process. It's in rewriting, I get serious about characters, description, introspection, etc. Here's a before and after scene from my book, *Chirp*:

Before: *As Blaze walked through the woods, the sun began to set.*

After: *As the sun set, a veil of deep purple draped the top of the forest like a new bride. Blaze loved this time of day when everything hushed and settled. Trees whispered their secrets, the wind gathered the world's wishes and carried them to Heaven.*

See what I mean by rough drafts being about just getting words/thoughts on the page? I knew I wanted her to walk through the woods, but in the first draft, I didn't give that scene the description it needed. Who knows? Before I'm done, I may rewrite the scene again.

Rewriting is the time to make changes. Add and delete scenes. Rearrange sentences. Move paragraphs. Let your character change his/her mind about something. Soften his/her tone in dialogue.

Read your chapters out loud because you use a different part of your brain when you listen to yourself. This will help you catch awkward sentences, missing words, and stiff dialogue. Also, many writers make the same mistakes over and over again, so become familiar with yours. In my first novel, I had someone grinning on every page. There are other things to watch for like confused words, too many ellipsis or em dashes, etc.

I just finished editing my current novel. When I finished, I'd cut 8500 words! When you edit, you should concentrate on cutting sentences as much as you can.

Avoid phrases like, as a matter of fact, one and only, each and every, in a manner of speaking, for all intents and purposes, for the most part, when it comes to, etc. unless you're using them in dialogue, then characters can be wordy and redundant!

EDITING

Nothing beats a good, professional editor, but there are some editing programs that will help you get your manuscript as perfect as possible before it goes to the editor—which can save you $$.

Each program works about the same, but navigating each is different. Listed below, are four I've used. I like *ProWritingAid* the best because it's easy to use, gives you a reason why they've made a suggestion, and checks for a lot of things. As of this writing, it runs $24-40 per year, depending on the package you want.
http://www.prowritingaid.com

AutoCrit is more difficult to navigate and costs $60-144 per year.
http://www.autocrit.com

Ginger sets up on your computer where you can approve the recommendations as it marks them in your manuscript. $59 per year.
http://www.ginger.com

Each of those three programs offers you the ability to copy and paste some of your work (limited word count) into their site to sample how it works.

What they check for:

Overused Words
Adverbs
Sentence Length
Writing Style
Clichés
Redundancies
Sticky Sentences
Consistency Errors
Comma Placement

Before purchase, make sure the program is compatible with your browser and word program.

Here are more helpful sites.

An online FREE tool. It requires no download and checks your manuscript for several things like repeat words, overuse of adverbs, passive voice, etc.
http://www.editminion.com

Another tool you might find helpful counts the words you use most in the text you submit. This helps eliminate overused words like it, took, just, etc.
http://www.wordcounter.com

Online proofing tool to help simplify your writing style.
http://www.hemingway.com

A spelling and grammar checking tool. Also sentence length and editing suggestions.
http://www.slickwrite.com

Free. Gives a detailed report of your text. Good entry level for new writers.
http://www.proofreadbot.com

Online plagiarism tool.
https://www.unplag.com

Language checker for spelling, style, and grammar. Free for personal use.
http://www.afterthedeadline.com

Oh, and don't overuse exclamation points!! And a personal pet peeve is using dialogue/attribution tags that aren't needed. Too many he said, she said, he asked, she asked slows the pace of the story. It's much better to identify your speaker through actions. If you must use a tag/attribution, the verb should follow the noun. John said, not, said John.

Many first time (fiction) authors think if they get an English teacher to go over their manuscript it counts as editing. That's only partially true. They can correct your grammar and punctuation, but you'll need so much more than technical help. You'll need an editor familiar with fiction writing. An editor who understands we don't always write complete sentences or use attributions each time a character speaks. If you're lucky enough to find an editor who can do it all, then hooray! If not, you may need several.

Ask other authors for recommendations. You can also find reputable editors on LinkedIn. Ask for references. Most editors will offer to edit a few pages or the first chapter for free to see if your personalities fit. This will also give you a chance to test communication with him/her.

Here's a site with advice about self-editing: https://marcustrowereditor.com/

And a great blog with advice about writing. http://theeditorsblog.net/

Types of Editors

Developmental/Substantive Editing
They identify plot holes, check for story threads that fizzle out, characters who fail to captivate, and secondary characters who aren't important to the story. They check voice, flow of action, and pacing.

Line Editing
They pay attention to sentence structure. Find awkward and sticky sentences. Does your story convey the right mood, emotion, and tone? They'll focus on overused words, ways to tighten your prose, redundancies, scenes that aren't necessary, use of cliché's, etc.

Copy Editing

This process is to check the technical side of the story. The editor will correct spelling, punctuation, and syntax. They'll pay attention to the rules of writing numbers, capitalization, hyphenation, and fonts. Did you write your character had green eyes in chapter one, but blue eyes in chapter sixteen? It's the job of this editor to find those mistakes.

Proofing

Proofreaders are the final step before publishing. Their job is to find any missing commas, spelling mistakes, typos, missing words, extra words, etc. They are technical readers looking for technical errors. They don't make suggestions for rearranging sentences or changing scenes or dialogue. All that has been done by editors prior to this process.

Keep in mind, **story trumps everything**. Readers will forgive a few errors and misplaced commas if the story is good.

COMMON MISTAKES

Characters All Sound the Same

Vary the rhythm of your dialogue. Most men don't talk as much as women, so make their dialogue less wordy. If you have a cop in your story, they speak in clipped dialogue.

Example:

Woman's dialogue:
Hanna opened her mouth to speak, but Tiffany waved her off. She was on a roll, and there was no stopping her. "I know what you're going to say. There's a calendar app." She flapped the air as if swatting mosquitos. "Sure there is, but I could get my own made and still make a ton of money. But I decided, heck, I should connect to my roots. Texas and Bluebird, so this is my original design."

Man's dialogue:
"Guilty. But still—didn't force you."
"Why? And what unfinished business could we possibly have?"
He ignored the question and whipped the truck into the drive-thru lane. "You want the Bluebird burger with mayo, no onions, no pickles and a vanilla coke. Right?"
She blinked. "You remember?"
He licked his lips. "I remember—*everything*."

Cop's dialogue:
Benny sat again. "So, after you called, I pulled up the file. Put it on a flash drive for you." He slid the small black stick across the desk. "The girl is twenty now. I'm surprised the stepmother is still pursuing this."
"Says she needs closure. Most people do."
"I guess. So, what do you want to know?"
"You didn't keep the case open long. I'm wondering why. No judgment. Just curious."

Recently, I read an unpublished novel that had a pimp in the story who never cursed. Unbelievable. I mean—I didn't believe the character because a pimp would at least say damn or hell now and then. Instead, he sounded like every other male character in the book.

Some writers have a hard time writing foul language, but if your character is an ex-con, like Rance, in my new adult romance, *Chirp*, his vocabulary should represent the six years he spent in prison. Remember, it's your character talking. Not you.

Play it Again Sam
Trust your reader. Don't repeat information. If you've covered it in dialogue, then don't say it again in narrative, and vice versa. If your hero/heroine frets about something in narrative and then has an occasion to relate that worry to someone, don't repeat it. Simply say something like—when he/she finished with the last detail, or when he/she ended the explanation, or have the receiving character comment regarding the info.

Info Dump

Large sections of narrative to give readers backstory. Most of the time all of that information can be spread throughout the story without slowing the pace. I have a multi-published writer friend who says to think of information like salt. Sprinkle it in, and the story will be better seasoned.

Check out the site below for a good exercise of how to convert backstory into character.
http://romanceuniversity.org/2016/05/27/converting-backstory-into-character-with-theresa-stevens-editor-2/

Where's Waldo?

Don't have your reader asking, "Where am I?" Put them in the same place as your character by showing location, time, surrounding. Use the five senses. However, if you have them in a room, don't bog the story down with so much description, the scene becomes about the furniture, other than the action.

Ready-Set-Action

A reaction always comes after an action.

The door swung wide when the wind gusted. Reaction/action—wrong
The wind gusted, and the door swung wide. Action/reaction—right

Her heart hammered when she saw him in the crowd. Reaction/action—wrong

When she saw him in the crowd, her heart hammered.
Action/reaction—right

The truck slid to a stop when she slammed on the brakes.
Reaction/action—wrong
She slammed on the brakes, and the truck slid to a stop.
Action/Reaction—right

It's All in Your Head
Your POV character is in charge of everything said and thought, so both should be written from his/her perspective, with the same voice. Don't have your narrative voice sound like a college professor if the POV character is uneducated.

FREQUENT PROBLEMS

Active and Passive Voice
If the subject of a verb does the action, the voice is active.

The <u>director</u> coached the actress.

If the subject gets the action, the voice is passive.

The actress was coached by the director.

Not all passive sentences are wrong, but in narrative, you should avoid them as much as possible.

Here are two good articles explaining active and passive voice.
https://www.butte.edu/departments/cas/tipsheets/style_purpose_strategy/active_passive.html
http://www.esf.edu/writingprogram/tipsheets/passive.htm

Point of View
What is POV? It's the person/character telling the story. It seems simple, but for most beginning authors, and even some experienced writers—it isn't. There are several types of POVs.

First Person POV
"I" tells the story using me, my, and mine.

I saw the sadness in Mary's eyes.

Second Person POV

The author tells the story through the reader's eyes using mostly you, your, and yours.

You saw the sadness in Mary's eyes.

Third Person POV

The author tells the story through a third party, using he/she, his/her, or their proper name.

He saw the sadness in Mary's eyes.

John saw the sadness in Mary's eyes.

Omniscient/Author's POV

The author tells the story through the thoughts of every character.

The link below provides clear descriptions of point of view.
http://www.dummies.com/education/literature/understanding-point-of-view-in-literature/

Over-Used Words

All
Almost
Anyway
As
Bad
Came
Could
Enter

Feel
Felt
Give/gave
Get/Got
Good
Hear/heard
It
Just
Know/knew
Like
Look
Pull
Push
Really
Saw
Seem
Seemed
Should
Showed
Smelled
So
Stood
That
Then
Think
Thought
Touch
Turn/turned
Very
Walk
Was/were

Went
Would

One of my last edits is to search for dreaded "ly" words that add nothing to a sentence. I'm not saying you should NEVER use one of these because sometimes it's a matter of style. And, using them in dialogue is always acceptable, unless overused.

If you use these, try reading your sentence without the "ly" word and see if it makes a difference in the meaning. They don't add information. For example, "The can was totally full of water." The meaning doesn't change if you say, "The can is/was full of water."

How about, "Deleting the adverb makes absolutely no difference." OR, "Deleting the adverb makes no difference." "He totally misunderstood the instructions." OR, "He misunderstood the instructions."

If your sentence makes sense without the "ly" word, delete it.

Absolutely
Actually
Basically
Certainly
Completely
Definitely
Literally
Probably
Totally
Virtually

Using began to, started to, etc. are two of my biggest problems. I use those a lot!! However, I've been taught a character doesn't begin or start to do anything. They just do it. She began to cry. She cried. He started to walk away. He walked away. Again, sometimes it's a matter of style, and hopefully, a reader won't put my book down if I use those.

Who or Whom?
Most times this rule will work.

If you can answer the question with, "he/she," then it's who.

If you can answer with, "him/her," then it's whom.

Who/whom went to the bank?
He went to the bank, so it's WHO went to the bank.

Who/whom did the panel choose?
They chose her, so it's WHOM did the panel choose.

~~WERDS~~ WORDS ARE HARD

You know the difference between *there, their*, and *they're*, but sometimes your fingers type the wrong one. I hate when that happens, but if I'm lucky, one of my online critique partners will find the mistake.

Once I wrote something about a man being viral. One of my readers pointed out unless he was sick, the word should be virile!

The bad news is spell check won't find those errors because they are all legitimate words. Just like they won't find any of these below.

Accept—to agree or receive or do
Except—not including

Advice—recommendations about what to do
Advise—to recommend something

Affect—influence something
Effect—to bring about a result

Allusion—indirect reference
Illusion—deception of reality

All ready—prepared
Already—by this time

Altar—a sacred table or railing in a church
Alter—to change

Altogether—completely
All together—unanimously

Ascent—climb
Assent—agreement

Awhile—(adverb) for a short time or period. It can't follow a preposition.
A while—(noun) a period or interval of time.

Bazaar—a market
Bizarre—strange

Brake—a device for stopping a moving vehicle
Break—to separate into pieces

Braun—a sir name
Brawn—muscular description

Breath—(noun) air inhaled or exhaled
Breathe—also to inhale or exhale, but used as a verb.

Breach—to break through or break a rule/contract
Breech—the back part of a gun barrel

Broach—to propose a subject for discussion
Brooch—a piece of jewelry

Canvas—a type of strong cloth
Canvass—to solicit votes

Capital—seat of government. Also financial resources.
Capitol—building in which the legislative body meets

Cite—refer to
Sight—the ability to see
Site—a location

Complement—round out or an addition that improves
something
Compliment—to praise or express approval

Conscience—sense of right and wrong
Conscious—awake

Council—a group of people who manage or advise
Counsel—advice

Dual—having two parts
Duel—combat between two people

Elicit—to draw or bring out
Illicit—not allowed by law

Eminent—well known, respected
Immanent—essential or fundamental
Imminent—about to happen

Envelop—to encircle or surround
Envelope—paper covering for letters or documents

Farther—measured greater physical distance
Further—something that is additional

Imitated—impersonate or mimic
Intimated—hint or imply

Its—of or belonging to it
It's—contraction of it and is

Lead—a type of metal
Led—past tense of "to lead"

Lie—to recline, lie down, or tell untruths
Lay—to place an object

Lose—unable to find
Loose—opposite of tight

Passed—past tense of "to pass"
Past—of a former time or place

Pedal—foot operated lever
Peddle—to sell goods

Precede—to come before
Proceed—to go forward

Principal—a head of authority
Principle—fundamental truth

Sell—deliver or exchange for money
Sale—transaction

Sole—one and only, individual, also bottom of a shoe
Soul—human, also refers to blues music

Stationary—standing still
Stationery—writing paper

Ann Everett

Than—introduces comparisons
Then—at that time or next

Their—possessive form of them
There—indicates a location or point
They're—contraction of "they are"

Through—into or out of; finished
Threw—past tense of throw
Thru—slang for through

To—in the direction of; to the extent of
Too—also or excessively
Two—a number

Virile—manly
Viral—infectious

Weather—describes the climate
Whether—introduces an alternative

Your—belonging to you
You're—contraction of "you are"

COMPOUND WORDS

There are three types of compound words:

Closed: haircut, eyelid, online
Open: car pool, high school, past tense
Hyphenated: follow-up, X-ray, U-turn

A handy hint I learned for figuring out if words should be hyphenated or not, is to read the sentence with each word individually, to see if it makes sense. If it doesn't, then use a hyphen.

Example: Pitch-black

She walked into a pitch room.
She walked into a black room.

Neither makes sense unless you are talking about the color of the room being black, so it needs a hyphen. She walked into a pitch-black room.

Let's try another one.

He pulled to the self gas pump.
He pulled to the service gas pump.
He pulled to the self-service gas pump.

Most of the time, for hyphens, that rule will work.

Some words that used to be open compound words have now become closed compound. That happens when two words are used together so much, they become one. Examples: website, online, backstory.

Also, depending on what part of speech the word is used for, like an adjective, adverb, or noun, the rule may change.

Example:

Everyday-adjective
Every day-adverb

And, to confuse matters more, sometimes, a word may be acceptable in two different forms. When in doubt, google it.

Here's a site with a list worth printing.
http://www.sightwordsgame.com/spelling/compound-words/

365 COMMONLY MISSPELLED WORDS

Absence

Acceptable

Accidentally

Accommodate

Accumulate

Achieve

Achievement

Acknowledge

Acquaintance

Acquire

Acquit

Acquitted

Adolescence

Advertise

Amateur

Among

Analysis

Analyze

Annual

Apartment

Apparatus

Apparent

Appearance

Arctic

Argue

Arguing

Argument

Arithmetic

Ascend

Atheist

Athlete

Athletic

Attendance

Awful

Awkward

Balance

Battalion

Beginning

Belief

Believe

Beneficial

Benefit

Benefited

Boundaries

Brilliant

Business

Camouflage

Category

Ceiling

Cemetery

Changeable

Chief

Choose

Chose

Collectible

Colonel

Column

Commission

Commitment

Committed

Committee

Comparative

Compelled

Competition

Conceit

Conceivable

Conferred

Conscience

Conscientious

Conscious

Consensus

Control

Controversial

Controversy	Discipline
Convenience	Dissatisfied
Criticize	Dormitory
Daiquiri	Easily
Decide	Ecstasy
Deferred	Eighth
Definite	Either
Definitely	Eligible
Definition	Eliminate
Describe	Embarrass
Description	Eminent
Desperate	Encourage
Develop	Encouragement
Dictionary	Encouraging
Difference	Environment
Dilemma	Equipped
Dining	Erroneous
Disappearance	Especially
Disappoint	Exaggerate
Disastrous	Excellent

Except	Generally
Exercise	Government
Exhilarate	Grammar
Exhilaration	Grandeur
Existence	Grateful
Experience	Grievous
Experiment	Guarantee
Explanation	Guidance
Familiar	Happiness
Fascinating	Harass
February	Height
Fiery	Heroes
Foreign	Hierarchy
Forfeit	Hindrance
Formerly	Humor
Forty	Humorous
Fourth	Hypocrisy
Frantically	Hypocrite
Fundamental	Identity
Gauge	Ignorance

Imaginary	Island
Imitation	Jealous
Immediately	Jewelry
Incidentally	Judgment
Incredible	Knowledge
Independent	Laboratory
Indispensable	Laid
Inevitable	Led
Inoculate	Leisure
Intellectual	Length
Intelligence	Lesson
Intelligent	Liaison
Interesting	Library
Interfere	License
Interpretation	Lieutenant
Interruption	Lightning
Invitation	Loneliness
Irrelevant	Lose
Irresistible	Losing
Irritable	Lying

Maintenance	Neighbor
Maneuver	Neither
Manufacture	Nineteen
Marriage	Ninety
Mathematics	Noticeable
Maybe	Occasion
Medicine	Occasionally
Medieval	Occurred
Memento	Occurrence
Mere	Official
Millennium	Often
Miniature	Omission
Minuscule	Omitted
Minute	Opinion
Mischievous	Opportunity
Misspelled	Optimism
Monastery	Optimistic
Mysterious	Ought
Naturally	Paid
Necessary	Parallel

Paralysis	Political
Paralyze	Possess
Particularly	Possession
Pastime	Possibility
Peculiar	Possible
Perceive	Practical
Perform	Practically
Performance	Precede
Permanent	Precedence
Permissible	Prefer
Perseverance	Preference
Persevere	Preferred
Personal	Prejudice
Personally	Preparation
Personnel	Presence
Perspiration	Prevalent
Persuade	Principal
Peruse	Principle
Physical	Privilege
Piece	Probably

Procedure	Realize
Proceed	Recede
Profession	Receipt
Professional	Receive
Professor	Receiving
Prominent	Recognize
Pronunciation	Recommend
Proof	Reference
Psychiatric	Referred
Psychiatry	Relevant
Psychology	Religious
Publicly	Repetition
Pursue	Restaurant
Quantity	Rhyme
Quarter	Rhythm
Questionnaire	Ridiculous
Queue	Sacrifice
Quiet	Sacrilegious
Quite	Salary
Quizzes	Schedule

Scissors

Secretary

Seize

Sense

Separate

Separation

Sergeant

Severely

Shining

Similar

Sincerely

Soldier

Sophomore

Specifically

Specimen

Statue

Stopping

Strength

Studying

Succeed

Successful

Succession

Supersede

Surely

Surprise

Technique

Temperamental

Temperature

Temporary

Tendency

Threshold

Toward

Tragedy

Transferring

Tries

Truly

Twelfth

Tyranny

Unanimous

Undoubtedly

Unnecessary

Until

Unusual

Using

Usually

Vacuum

Village

Villain

Weather

Weird

Whether

TENSES

I talk in mixed tenses, so I write the same way. Not good, so I'm told. For a better understanding of them, here's a brief description.

Verbs determine when something happens, in the present, in the past, or in the future. They set the tense of your tale. Here are some examples:

Present tense—I/you/we/they drink --he/she/it drinks

Past tense—I/you/he/she/it/we/they drank

Future tense—I/you/he/she/it/we/they will drink

Present perfect tense—I/you/he/she/it/we/they have drunk

Past perfect tense—I/you/he/she/it/we/they had drunk

Future perfect tense—I/you/he/she/it/we/they will have drunk

Go here for an article about using the right tense. It also has a quiz to test your knowledge.
http://www.ecenglish.com/learnenglish/lessons/past-simple-or-past-perfect

The following links have good information.
http://www.dailywritingtips.com/5-lessons-for-mixing-past-and-present-tense/

http://depts.washington.edu/engl/askbetty/tenses.php

NUMBERS IN FICTION

Use numerals for street numbers, page numbers, decimals, percentages, dates, and hours followed by A.M or P.M.
1602 Magnolia Street
The main character first appears in Chapter 1, page 12.
34 115th Street
The pipe is 50 inches in diameter.
The scarf was reduced 25 percent.
June 2, 1967. But if you use a date *without* the year, then you may use st, nd, rd, or th with the number. June 2nd, October 3rd, April 4th, January 1st.
They arrived at the theater at 1:15 p.m. In narrative, use numbers for exact time. In dialogue, use words.

Spell out numbers for *amounts* (not ages) less than one hundred.
She spent thirty-nine dollars for a casserole dish.

Over one hundred, use numerals.
My parents live 1,224 miles away.

When numbers are used with million, billion, etc. the above rules still apply.
The country has a population of six million. (Six is less than one hundred)
The citizens collected 232 million pennies for cancer awareness. (232 is more than one hundred)
In writing fiction, words should be used in place of symbols, both in dialogue and narrative.
Percent, not %

Number, not #
Dollar, not $

Don't use abbreviations for pounds, ounces, feet, inches, yards, hours, seconds, or miles per hour. Spell the words out.

Spell out numbers that begin a sentence.
Four hundred pumpkins were delivered to the market.

Writing Ages

To hyphenate or not to hyphenate? That is the question. I still have to look this up because I can't remember the rule, so here it is.
If the age is used as an adjective before a noun, you use a hyphen.

The 13-year-old boy made a touchdown.
My 21-year-old sister sings beautifully.

NOT when stating an *age*.

He is 13 years old.
My sister is 21 years old.

Amounts

Hyphenate compound numbers from twenty-one to ninety-nine.
She owned fifty-four pairs of shoes.
She collected two hundred and thirty-six dollars for charity.

Spell out simple fractions and hyphenate them.
Mary took one-half of the peaches.

She needed two-thirds cups of sugar for the recipe.

Don't hyphenate for a span of time.
Their vacation lasted from July 15 through August 1.

If writing numbers side by side, write one as a number and one as a word to avoid confusion.
She bought 10 fifty-pound crates of peaches.

Phone numbers should be written as numerals.
1-555-432-5555

Spell out heights.
She was five-two in her stocking feet. She was five feet two.*
She was five feet two inches tall.*

*If these numbers preceded a noun, then they would need a hyphen like in the first example and the one below.
A five-foot-three girl burst into the room.

For questions concerning the rules of writing, I suggest you purchase a copy of *The Chicago Manual of Style*, which is what most professional editors' use.

Also, a great blog covering how to write numbers and other subjects.
http://www.theeditorsblog.net/2013/01/13/numbers-in-fiction/

ITALICS

Italicize titles of books, newspapers, magazines, careful not to include the word "the" unless it is part of the title.

The Red Badge of Courage (book)
the *Mount Pleasant Daily Tribune* (newspaper)
Southern Living (magazine)

Versions of the Bible or individual books are not italicized. However, individually titled editions are.

The New Oxford Annotated Bible

Italicize names of ships, aircraft, works of art, (paintings, sculptures, photographs) and movies.

The *Titanic* (ship)
Enola Gay (aircraft)
The Last Supper (painting)
Toy Story (movie)

Also *italicize* **TV shows, radio shows, plays, operas, ballets, long poems, and symphonies (title of musical piece), journals, pamphlets, reports, podcasts, blogs. Also titles of comic strips and cartoons.**

Modern Family (TV show)
Amos and Andy (radio show)
Cabaret (play)
Carmen (opera)
Paradise Lost (long poem)
Symphony No. 1, in C major, op. 21 (symphony) Notice only the title is in italics, and not the generic description.
Nature Protocols (journal)

Common Sense (pamphlet)
The Nerdist (podcast)
Gawker (blog)

Letters referred to as letters are italicized.
On the map, *X* marked the spot.
Mississippi has four *s*'s in it. For plural, only the letter itself is italicized, not the apostrophe or following s.

Odd sounds should be italicized.
Squish-squish. Whomp-whomp.

There is a lot of controversy concerning how to write internal thoughts. I prefer to use italics without an attribution/tag. Some use italics with an attribution. Some write the thought in narrative with no special focus.

If he only knew the truth.
If he only knew the truth, she thought.
If he only knew the truth.

For me, the first example is best. By using italics, I know that is the character's thought without saying it's her thought—as shown in the second example.

The third choice is used by some authors because they feel when you're in a character's point of view, then everything—dialogue, narrative, and thoughts are from that character, so nothing needs to be italicized.

I think all the examples are acceptable. Decide what works best for you and be consistent.

COULDA-WOULDA-SHOULDA

Here in Texas, we're known for slaughtering the King's English. We say idn't instead of isn't. Gonna in place of going to. Give me becomes gimme. Fixin' to instead of about to. And you can't be Texan unless you throw in y'all!

If you write a Texas or southern character, I recommend you keep the natural slang to a minimum. Maybe you have one character who uses those terms, but mostly, I'd stick to proper spelling. It bogs the reader down to read so much slang—even those of us who speak that way!

I say coulda, woulda, shoulda, which in my mind translates to "could of, would of, should of," but those are incorrect uses of the verb phrases, could have, would have, and should have.

If you use an excess of slang, I recommend doing a word search within your document to see how many you have. I end up changing quite a few back to proper English. I've also learned other parts of the country say the same idiom slightly different than we do in the Lone Star. Here, we say—she was drunk on her butt. Other regions say—she was drunk *off* her butt.

We say, three sheets in the wind vs. three sheets to the wind.
Put it up vs. put it away
Turn it out vs. turn it off
A wreck vs. a car accident
Coke vs. soda

Ann Everett

Buggy vs. shopping cart

The general rule is to write dialogue anyway you choose, but in narrative you need to follow the rules.

Here are a few examples of when to use what.

Fewer—a smaller number.
Less—a smaller amount.

Can—has the ability.
May—has permission.

Who—refers to he or she.
Whom—refers to him or her.

Former—happened in the past.
Latter—happens after another event.

CAPITALIZATION

Capitalize names of people, races, nationalities, places, organizations, and sometimes things.
Tom, Tom Jones, Mr. Jones, Grandpa Jones.
American, Cuban, African-American.
Canadian, English, Latin.
Disney World, Jack's Crab Shack, Austin, Texas.
Mothers Against Drunk Driving, Supreme Court, Democrats.

Days, months, holidays, but not seasons.
Monday, June, Christmas.
winter, spring, summer, fall—unless part of a title.

Religious terms with *sacred* significance.
God
God the Father
the Virgin
Savior/Saviour
Heaven
He, His and Him should be capitalized when referring to God.
the Bible
The Good Book
Buddha
Koran
Books of the Bible: Genesis, Exodus, Acts, etc.

Do not capitalize a nonspecific use of god.
He looked like a god.

Titles paired with names.
Reverend Jackson
President Washington

But not when used as a name.
The president will speak tonight.
The pastor will pray for the sick.
Aunt Mary.
Aunt Mary will be here at seven.
But not here: My aunt Mary will be here at seven.

Brand names and trademarks are tricky.
Ipad or iPad?
EBay or eBay?
I write it as the trademark appears iPad and eBay.
Google as a noun is capitalized. But as a verb, *I googled that*, isn't.
IBM, Ford, Dr. Pepper, Microsoft Word

DIRECTIONS

If North, South, East, and West are used as sections of the country, then they need a capital. If they are used as directions, then no capital is needed.
I've lived in the West for ten years.
The restaurant is four blocks south of Main Street.

Major words in titles of books, articles, and songs, but not the, a, or an, unless they are the first word.
Two Wrongs Make a Right
The Catcher in the Rye
Tell Me a Secret

Wars and Battles

Korean War
World War Two
Civil War

Schools, museums, and colleges
Texas Tech University
Fowler Elementary School
The High Museum
Houses of worship
Tennyson Methodist Church
the Cathedral of St. Paul

DO NOT CAPITALIZE

School subjects unless they have a number or name a language
math, science, history
Math 101, English, Spanish

Careers
My dad is a dentist.

Animals
cat, dog, cow

Plants
elm tree, grass, shrub

If used with a proper adjective, then capitalize the adjective, but not the plant.
English ivy, Kentucky bluegrass

Same goes for musical instruments
piano, horn, guitar
French horn, Spanish guitar

I've just touched on some of the basic writing rules. Again, I strongly suggest you get a copy of *The Chicago Manual of Style.*

TWELVE TIPS FOR DEVELOPMENTAL SELF-EDITING

1. Have a strong opening sentence

I like to think the first sentence in my book sets the tone of the story. Even if it is a murder mystery, I want the reader to understand there will be humor and romance.

First line of *Laid Out and Candle Lit*
Not only did Tizzy Donovan think her cup was always half empty, she was pretty sure someone had spit in it.

From *You're Busting My Nuptials*
Twenty-four hours ago Tizzy Donovan was naked in Ridge Cooper's bed, screaming to get God's attention.

From *Tied With a Bow and No Place to Go*
Jay Roy Hobbs held the county record for talking women out of their panties.

From *Tell Me a Secret*

According to scientific studies, Maggie knew even good girls got aroused by bad boys.

2. Each chapter should end with a hook. Something to make the reader turn the page.

Raynie's hands trembled as she gazed at divorce papers.

"As soon as the weather clears, I want you to leave. Until then, stay out of my way."

"Do you think Mr. Kincaid is her dad?"

"I don't know. But if he isn't, I'd be willing to bet he knows who is."

3. Can readers identify with your characters?

Your characters shouldn't be perfect. They are much more interesting if they have flaws and quirks.

A small town deputy who day trades.
A tarot card reader who dresses like a modern day gypsy.
An awkward girl with a word of the day fetish.

4. You must have conflict.

In *Tell Me a Secret,* Jace and Maggie are opposites.

Jace has the perfect family.
Maggie has a non-existent relationship with her mother and no idea who her father is.

Jace is a player.
Maggie avoids men because of her mother's promiscuous behavior.

Both characters must change for a romance to develop.

Hero and heroine must have attainable goals and achieve them against all odds.

The push and pull of the struggle moves the story forward.

6. Narrative/introspection

You have to get inside your character's head to let the reader "in" on his/her thoughts. This is where you can show his/her true colors in spite of how he/she is acting. It is through these "inner" thoughts you let the reader be privy to what the characters don't know yet, thus engaging the reader in your story even more.

7. POV

As you self-edit, check to make sure you didn't "head-hop" and slip from one character's head to another. This pertains mostly to third person POV. In another section, I give examples of POV, and links that will help you understand the different types.

8. Dialogue

If all your characters sound alike, you need to change them. Men talk less and in clipped sentences, whereas women are much wordier! You can give a character a catchphrase that will identify them the minute they speak. In my series, I have a sheriff who starts a lot of sentences with "God Almighty." When the reader comes to that, they know who the speaker is without an attribution/tag.

9. Trust your reader

Don't keep beating your reader over the head by repeating information you've already revealed. If you give background info about your character being an only child, your reader will remember, so don't keep reminding them.

10. Surprise!

To keep your reader engaged, throw something unexpected into the mix. In *Tell Me a Secret*, someone dies. My critique partners said, "Wow, we did not see that coming." That's a good thing because it kept them turning the page!

11. Show don't tell

Lord, how many times are you going to hear this? About a zillion. Why? Because long paragraphs of exposition and backstory bogs your story down. Yes, you will need some here and there, but it is better to work all that info in via dialogue or short paragraphs of introspection. Ask yourself—does your reader need to know all that? Is it important to the story? To the development of the character? If it isn't, then cut it. Believe it or not, you may cut entire chapters. I have.

Another form of telling is the use of adverbs in dialogue tags.

Here's an excerpt from my writer's reference book, *Body Language, A Quick Reference for Character Action and Description.*

Use as few adverbs as possible. I recommend not using them at all in dialogue tags.

There should never be a reason to tag dialogue this way: *She screamed angrily.* If you write her reaction (red face, fisted hands, gritted teeth, etc.) to whatever made her angry, you've shown she's mad, and the word *angrily* is not needed.

I recently ~~read~~ tried to read a book which had an adverb with every dialogue tag. "I couldn't do it!" I said excitedly. I'm not kidding. The author used just about every adverb known to man. She said wistfully. She said softly. She said joyfully. She said happily. She said cheerily. Knowingly. Heartily. Anxiously. Uncertainly. And the list went on and on.

Tagging with adverbs, in my humble opinion, is lazy writing. Look for ways to *show* those emotions, so the reader experiences the same thing the character does. It's much more effective to have your character's eyes sparkle or widen, have her bounce on her toes, dance around the room, scream, holler, or elevate her voice. Give the reader those actions, and there's no need for, *said joyfully, happily, cheerily.*

12. Don't be preachy.

Have you ever read a story where a character asks another about a political race? Then the character who responds climbs onto his soap box. Don't use your story as a platform to express your personal views. Do that in your blogs.

In fiction, readers want to be entertained, not sermonized. If an issue is an integral part of the story and you have a character who is an activist, of course, he'll preach. But be careful, because forcing a personal view will turn most readers off. Now, didn't I sound preachy? Yeah, see what I mean?

Jacqui Murray's WordDreams blog has articles on How to Describe Nature, 51 Great Similes to Spark Imagination, and 65 Ways to Describe Sight and Eyes in Your Writing, just to name a few. Check out her site. https://worddreams.wordpress.com/writers-tips/

ALWAYS back up your files and photos on a flash/thumb drive. Each time you make changes to your manuscript, back the file up again. This way, if something goes wrong and your computer crashes, you'll have your files! I back everything up on a flash drive.

BEFORE YOU PUBLISH

Branding and platform are two words you'll hear all the time in the Author World. So this is my take on what they mean. I feel they pertain more to non-fiction writers. What are you about? What are you selling?

If I mention Suze Orman, you immediately think of financial advice. Bill O'Reilly, political commentary. Those are their brands and platforms. You probably wouldn't be interested in reading a young adult novel written by either of them because they have no association with that genre.

For fiction writers, it's much harder. Sure, I write romance, but I also write light mysteries. So how do I fit those into my brand and platform? The best I can do is be consistent in my writing style. That's my brand and platform.

Ann Everett. Sass, sizzle, suspense…Texas style.

Sass…I always have at least one quirky, snarky character.

Sizzle…there will be steamy sex.

Suspense…may have a bit of mystery.

Texas style…because all my stories take place in the Lone Star State…cuz that's where I'm from.

Regardless of what you think brand or platform means, it boils down to making emotional connections with people. To come up with your brand/platform, you need to ask yourself these questions:

Who am I?
What do I write?
How do I convey that in a short tagline?

A logo is helpful.

Then plaster it everywhere. On bookmarks, social media headers, Website, etc.

You can get help with ideas by searching for "logo designers." Cost can be as little as $10.

In addition to establishing your brand/platform, other things need to be in place before you publish your first book.

Website

There are sites you can get for free, but keep in mind, if you use a free site, everything you post on it belongs to them. They can share those posts anywhere and anytime they choose. I suggest you invest the $$ and get a professional website done. I can recommend http://www.rocksteadysolutions.com Owner, Janis McAdoo is reasonable and super easy to work with. More than anything, your site needs to be mobile friendly! A good designer will make sure of that.

Check out these sites for inspiration.
http://www.noraroberts.com/
http://www.victoriascott.com/

http://jodyhedlund.com/
http://www.jgrisham.com/
http://stephenking.com/

Take time to set up a Globally Recognized Avatar. Each time you leave a comment on a WordPress blog, your chosen gravatar will appear.

http://www.todaymade.com/blog/gravatar-in-wordpress/

Pages to Consider

About me/bio page—Here is the place to tell all about yourself. How you got started writing, how many dogs or cats you have, any awards you've won, etc. It's a good idea to write more than one bio and keep the choices in a word document file. Google doesn't like for you to use the same bio everywhere. Not sure why, but it affects the indexing. I don't know enough about how the web works to explain it, but I know it makes a difference. If you guest blog or promote on other sites, some of those blogger/promoters will ask you to send an "original" bio, different from the one you typically use. So it's good to have several ready when asked.

Here's a 75-word bio of mine.

Native Texan, Ann Everett, lives on a small pond where she writes, bakes, and fights her addiction to Diet Dr. Pepper.
Ten useless facts about Ann:
Married her high school sweetheart.

Loves shopping at thrift stores.
Doesn't remember her first kiss.
Hates talking on the telephone.
A really sharp pencil makes her happy.
Secretly wants to get a tattoo.
Still trying to figure out how she made the National Honor Society in high school.
Thankful wrinkles aren't painful.
Sucks at math.

This one is more professional and 164 words.

Award winning and Amazon Best-Selling author, Ann Everett embraces her small town upbringing and thinks Texans are some of the funniest people on earth. When speaking at conferences and to writing groups, businesses, book clubs, and non-profit organizations, she incorporates her special brand of wit, making her programs on marketing, self-publishing, and the benefits of laughter, informative and fun.

Her short stories have appeared in The Green Silk Journal, Snag Today, and Story Teller Magazine.

A member of Northeast Texas Writers' Organization and a top reviewer on thenextbigwriter.com, she lives on a small lake in Northeast Texas, where she writes, bakes, and fights her addiction to Diet Dr. Pepper.

She's been featured on:
Proud of East Texas with Joan Hallmark, KLTV-TV, Tyler, Texas

East Texas Live, KETK-TV, Tyler, Texas
KTSS-TV, Hope, Arkansas
The Authors Show with Don McCauley, Internet radio show
The Chandler & Brownsboro Statesman, Chandler, Texas
The Daily Tribune, Mt. Pleasant, Texas
Tyler Morning Telegraph, Tyler, Texas
InMagazine, East Texas

For bio ideas, check these out.

https://debbiemacomber.com/
http://jayneannkrentz.com/biography/

You'll also need a headshot. One in color, and one in black and white. B&W for printed material, color for online. If you're self-publishing, you don't want to include a color photo inside your book, because that will put it into a color category, and you'll be charged a higher per page cost each time the book is printed. You can put a color photo on the outside back cover, and it won't affect your cost.

Book page—A place to show off the covers of all your books along with their blurb/summary, which should be about 200 words. I recommend you write a longer one (400-600 words) to have on hand. For future promotion, some sites will ask for a summary different from the one you use on the cover.

Let's talk about writing the back cover summary/blurb. For me, it's as hard as writing the book! Taking 80,000+

words and condensing the story into a 200-word description, along with introducing your main characters and their conflict without giving away too much.

I like to read back copy from best-selling authors who write in the same genre as I. That way, I get a feel for how they cut their story down to so few words.

Don't expect your first draft/attempt to be the final result. You may have to rewrite a dozen times before you get it the way you like. But it's worth the effort. Why? Because according to my personal research among readers, it's the number one influence that determines if they buy the book. The cover came in second.

Your website book page is also the place to include endorsements you've gotten from professional review sites, or famous authors/people. These testimonials are important because on some promo sites, like BookBub, they will help you get accepted. If you know a NYT or USA best-selling author, ask them to write a two sentence endorsement of your book. It's worth a shot because all they can say is no.

Events page—This is where you'll list all your upcoming book signings, speaking engagements, book festivals, interviews, personal appearances, etc.

Media page—Show all the press you've received. TV and radio coverage. Newspaper articles, any photos from events or bookstore/library appearances. This could also be included on your events page in place of having its own page.

Blog—If you plan to blog, this is the place to do it. You can link it to Goodreads or other sites. Each time you post, the blog will automatically appear on those sites.

You'll also need a "call to action" which means you ask visitors to join your email list, or even better, offer them something for subscribing. Maybe it's free short stories, or a sample of your next book, or writing tips.

Social media icons should be linked and displayed so that anyone reading your blog can easily share, friend, and follow you.

A contact form should be included.

Now, what to blog about?

1. Interview other authors
2. Write an article about writing. Tips, hints, etc.
3. Write about results you got from an ad campaign.
4. Find quotes from other author's books and blog about them. Ten Funny Quotes. Ten Amazing Quotes. Ten Best Risqué Quotes. Don't forget to add a visual.
5. If one of your characters has a special interest in cooking, gardening, fashion, etc., let them blog about that.

A great way to market is to comment on other bloggers posts. This will get your name and website in front of other commenters. Or, maybe you'd like to guest blog. Check out these sites for opportunities.

Provides the leads if you want to furnish a blog or need a blog for your site.
http://www.BloggerLinkUp.com

Submit your blog. They decide if it's a good fit. If yes, they publish it on the site.
http://www.MyBlogGuest.com

Connect with the right bloggers for their projects or campaigns.
http://www.Blogdash.com

Blogs are listed by category, making it easy to connect with other specialty sites. Pitch ideas or receive pitches.
http://www.guestr.com

Be sure to set up Google Alerts for your favorite search terms.
http://www.googlealerts.com

Displays all the headlines of the latest stories from the best sites and blogs. Submit your own site here.
http://www.alltop.com

Don't forget to contact individual bloggers for guest blogging prospects.

Social Media
If you don't already have social media profiles, create those. It's overwhelming, but choose three you like most and concentrate on spending time with them each day.

Facebook
Twitter
Google+
Pinterest
LinkedIn
Instagram
YouTube

Each site will need a profile created listing your website URL. That way, people can go there from any of the social sites. More on that later.

Create an author profile on Goodreads.
https://www.goodreads.com/author/program

Create an author profile/page on Amazon (author central)
https://www.authorcentral.amazon.com/gp/help

This is also a good time to join Facebook groups that relate to your books. Although you want to engage with other writers to share information and experiences, you *really* want to connect with readers. However, don't use social media to post—buy my book, buy my book, buy my book! It's more effective to post informative articles, humorous quotes, interesting photos, tips, questions, etc. People who respond to such posts will want to know more about you and visit your website, where they will see your books!

When is it okay to promote your book on social media? When you have a reduced price or free offer, a new release, a contest, a Facebook party with prizes, teasers leading up to the release, etc. You're still saying "buy my book," but in a more creative way.

You can do your own FB party or have a party organizer do it. I recommend an organizer. Many tour companies offer FB party packages.

To find Facebook groups, use the search bar to explore the choices. For me, I would type, readers of romance, readers of contemporary romance, readers of new adult romance, and readers of Texas romance. Before you request to join a group, check out what they are posting. If all they do is promote one book after another, they won't be beneficial to you. What you should look for is a chance to build relationships.

To do that, you should *like, share, and comment* on their posts. Remember, they don't have to be about books. They can be about animals, cooking, photography, etc. Getting to know someone takes time. Once they "know" you, chances are they'll want to see what you write without you screaming, "Buy my book."

The most important thing concerning social media is to be consistent. Set aside time every day to post on FB and Twitter. They even have sites where you can schedule your post, and they'll post for you!

http://www.hootsuite.com
http://www.buffer.com

Find the right hashtags to use to locate readers of your genre. You can use Twitter's search functions or here are two sites that will help. Use those hashtags when promoting your books. This will also help find readers to follow who enjoy reading your genre. I've been told to use a hashtag for keywords, not just on FB or Twitter, but everywhere. Not a bad idea.

http://www.TwiTag.com
http://www.Hashtags.org

Find the most popular hashtag usage patterns at:
http://hashtagify.me/

BETA READERS

Beta readers aren't editors or proofreaders, but they are valuable in telling you what works and doesn't work in your story.

What is a beta reader? A reader who will read your book in a short amount of time, so they get a sense of pace, flow, and characters. They'll pick up on things as minor as characters having names too old for their age. Or a character who has been a ballroom dancer going out to a dance club in flats instead of heels.

Even a mistake that small will make your story less believable. So get good betas and pay attention to what they say! I almost always use every suggestion they offer.

Goodreads has several groups of beta readers. Post a request there, and you'll get responses.

PUBLISH

TYPES OF PUBLISHING/PROS AND CONS

Traditional (big house)
You pitch an agent. They sell your manuscript to a publisher.

Pros
They take care of everything. Cover, formatting, title, editing.

If you become a top seller for them, they'll provide a publicist who will arrange public appearances and speaking engagements. They'll draft press releases and create and distribute promotional materials.

You'll get an advance, for a first time unknown author, $2500-$5000. Or, if you have a successful blog with a huge following, your advance can increase up to $10,000 or more. (This is usually for non-fiction books, where a blogger blogs about cooking, fashion, self-help, etc.)

Cons
Long wait time until the book is published.

Deadlines to meet.

Most authors don't earn out their advance.

If the "first run" of your book doesn't sell-out within approximately 90 days, the publisher won't be interested in your next book, even if it is a series.

You will make about 10% of each book sold until your advance "earns out."

The publisher won't do any marketing for you, other than getting your book on shelves in bookstores.

You have no true way of checking your sales. Only the publisher's word.

Requires a contract, during which time you might not be able to publish anywhere else.

Rejection letters.

Publishers could ask for an advance back if the book doesn't sell as expected. Check your contract for that stipulation.

So, how do you find an agent?

There's a whole book full of them. *Guide to Literary Agents*. Make a list of 4-8 who appeal to you, then polish up that query and send it their way. However...

One of the best ways is to attend conferences that feature agents in your genre who accept samples prior to the conference date. Then on the day of, schedule a meeting with the agent you submitted to.

This will give you 15-20 minutes of face time with them in which you'll get valuable info about your work and find out if they're interested in reading more. If they do or not, the experience will be helpful.

To find conferences near you, do an online search. OR, attending a conference in another state makes a nice vacation!

Small Press
Pitch directly to them.

Pros
Don't need an agent.

Acceptance is easier.

Develop a personal relationship.

They do everything for you, (you even get input sometimes) cover, formatting, editing, etc.

No cost to you.

Cons
No advance.

Books not in bookstores.

No marketing.

No true way of checking sales. (Only their word)

Requires a contract during which you may not be allowed to publish anywhere else.

Kindle Scout

Pros
Submit directly to them.

If chosen, receive $1500 advance.

Editing provided.

They market within Amazon and other places.

50/50 royalty split.

Paid each month.

Cons
Must sign a 5-year contract.

Vanity Press

YOU pay them to publish your book.

Pros
NONE

Cons
They charge to publish your book, sometimes through the back door by not asking for any money up front, but pay you nothing until your book covers their cost of publishing. Guess what? You have no way of knowing what that cost is or when your book sales cover it. You only have their word.

Vanity publishers make their money from the publishing fee you pay, and the books you order.

No matter how much they praise your work or tell you what a fantastic writer you are or promise you the moon—don't sign a contract with these folks…unless, it is a reputable company like Bookbaby.com.

Self/Indie Publish

Pros
Publish for free in print and eBook on CreateSpace and Kindle.
Receive free ISBN from CreateSpace, or you can buy your own from Bowker.
Access to daily sales. Kindle updates hourly.
Complete control.
Do it yourself and spend no money.
Get to keep up to 70% of royalty.

Publishers watch Amazon sales, so if your book becomes a bestseller, and you want to be traditionally published, chances are, they will come to you with an offer.

Cons

Because it's easy, everyone is doing it.

According to *Forbes Magazine,* over 80,000 books per month are published, so your chance of success is slim.

Most authors only sell an average of 250 books. If you can't DIY, you'll spend money for cover, formatting, editing, etc. (my average cost is about $300 per book)

You must do your own marketing.

Audio Books

I've used ACX (Audiobook Creation Exchange) for two of my books. This is also an Amazon company. This is how it works:

1. Confirm you have the rights to your book.
2. Create a profile.
3. Find a producer by listening to samples of narration and ask them to audition.
4. Review the auditions you receive.
5. Make a deal. ACX offers two ways of producing a book. Narrators/producers either agree to a 50/50 royalty split, where you pay no money but share any sales royalty with the narrator/producer. OR, they charge per hour, and you keep 100% of the royalty. I did a 50/50 split with both my books.
6. Get started.
7. Approve the final product
8. Distribute

9. Promote

10. Earn royalties

If you have a book that has sold well, Amazon will offer a stipend to producers. This gives producers an incentive to narrate your book. The second book I published with ACX, had been a bestseller on Amazon, so they offered $100 per hour stipend up to 8 finished hours of recording. That allowed me to get the narrator I wanted most.

Go to http://www.acx.com for all the details.

You will need to sign a contract. You will also get 25 free copies for US distribution, and 25 free copies for UK distribution. This will help you get reviews.

The site below will advertise those free copies for you for $10. I used the site and was pleased with the results. Be sure and watch their video about gifting the audio book instead of just sending the code. If you send the code, the recipient can download ANY book. You don't want that. You want to make sure they get YOUR book so you might get a review from it.
http://audiobookboom.com/authors

There is another site I recently learned about, which is, http://www.findaway.com

They also do audiobooks with distribution, but that's all I know about them. You can go to their website for all the information.

AMAZON PROGRAMS

Kindle Direct Publishing
You publish on Kindle for free and receive a 35% royalty with a non-exclusive contract.

Kindle Direct Publishing Select
If enrolled in the KDP Select program, Amazon offers several tools for authors to promote their books, and since they are the biggest book seller in the universe, it would be a mistake not to take advantage of their advertising opportunities.

During your KDP Select contract, you can't sell your book, give it away, or post more than an excerpt anywhere, not even on your website. This applies to digital books only. You can still do whatever you want with your print book.

Here's how it works and what you get.

- Automatically renews every 90 days (can be edited to not have auto renewal.)
- Higher royalties: 70% instead of 35% but you have to select the percentage.
- Promo deals: Countdown deals and free book promos.
- Automatically enrolls you in the Kindle Unlimited and Kindle Owner's Lending Library.
- Kindle Owner's Lending Library gives you the opportunity to receive a share of the Kindle Select Global Fund that pays authors based on number of

pages read (the amount you receive changes every month, depending on the size of the Global Fund.)

I have my eBooks enrolled in KDP Select which means I sell my eBooks on Amazon exclusively, (required to join the program.) I do this because I make a larger royalty on each book and it puts me into the KENP program where I get paid for each page read by readers who borrow my book.

Some authors complain about this program because the royalty paid changes each month, but the way I look at it…readers in this program (KU) are people who will NEVER buy my book. Why should they spend $$ on it, when there are millions of other books they can borrow? By being in the KENP program, I'm tapping into a market I would otherwise miss. Just my opinion.

Kindle Unlimited (KU)
This is a subscription program through Amazon that allows readers to borrow books for a monthly fee. Currently, I think it's $10 per month.

Kindle Edition Normalized Page Count (KENPC)
Shows the tally of pages read for each of your loaned books.

You're not in it for the money
You just want to write. You're not in it for the money. Yeah. Not until you make some! Then it will be all about the money. And it should be, to a degree. Even though you're doing something you love, your time is valuable.

Treat it like a business. If you don't, no one else will. The truth is, most of your family and friends (who don't write) probably think of it as your hobby.

RESPONSIBILITIES OF AN INDIE AUTHOR

Cover design

Our brains process images 60,000 times faster than text, so we need to make sure we have a great image on our cover. Couples on romance books outsell those that have random images. And, having a dude without a shirt on the cover is even better!

You want an image that is high resolution, and on sites where you purchase stock photos, the cost will run on average around $20-$30 each.

If you write a series or companion books, consider similar cover designs.

Plain fonts and clip art might make a potential buyer think if the author spent no time on their cover, then maybe they didn't spend much honing their craft!

Where do you get those great images, and how much to they cost? Well, the good news is you can get some fantastic photos for free. The bad news is a lot of those sites aren't searchable—meaning they aren't in categories, so you have to spend a good amount of time looking through hundreds before you find the one you want. Many of the photos will be more applicable to blog postings or memes than covers.

Double check each listing **to make sure photos are free from copyright restrictions or license under Creative Commons Public Domain.

Creative Commons Zero means you can copy, modify, distribute, and use the work for personal or commercial purposes in any way you choose without asking permission.

Creative Commons with Attribution means you can use the photos in any way you like as long as you credit the creator of the photo. It's also recommended to include the creator's link to his/her site if they have one listed.

A lot of sites may have restrictions about sharing images with someone else. Sending the image you downloaded for free to a third party may be prohibited. Please check each site's license for restrictions.

**I, Ann Everett, claim no responsibility for any misinformation/mistakes concerning these site listings. It is YOUR responsibility to read each site's rules and regulations.

Death to Stock Photos
(http://www.deathtothestockphoto.com/)
Sign up, and each month you'll receive a pack of 10 photos delivered to your inbox. Be sure and read their license requirements for usage.

Epicantus (http://www.epicantus.tumblr.com/)
This site offers free original photography by Daria.
Searchable: yes
Attribution: check site

Flickr/Creative commons
(https://www.flickr.com/creativecommons/)
This site has over 100 million Creative Commons licensed images. Just be sure to read the different CC licenses, so you know which is best for you and the way you intend to use the image.
Searchable: No
Attribution: Check license

Freeimages (http://www.freeimages.com/)
Features a large selection of categories.
Searchable: Yes
Attribution: Check individual photos.

Freerange Stock (http://www.freerangestock.com/)
This is a free community service where members can browse, download photos for personal or commercial use. They also offer photo tutorials.
Searchable: Yes
Attribution: Appreciated

Freestocks (http://www.freestocks.org/)

Getrefe (http://www.GetRefe.com/)
Lots of scenery photos and they have a free section.
Searchable: Yes
Attribution: Check license

Gratisography (http://www.gratisography.com/)
Some of the most unusual, zaniest photos you'll find. All photographed by Ryan McGuire, artist and web designer.

Searchable: Yes
Attribution: No

IM Free (http://imcreator.com/free)
Doesn't offer as many selections as other sites, but the photos are great quality.
Searchable: Yes
Attribution: Yes

Jay Mantri (http://www.jaymantri.com/)
Inspiring photos updated weekly.
Searchable: No
Attribution: Check license

Kaboom Pics (http://www.kaboompics.com/)
Wide variety of free stock photos that can be used for commercial purposes but cannot be sold or redistributed. New pictures added daily.
Searchable: Somewhat
Attribution: Appreciated

Life of Pix (http://www.lifeofpix.com/)
Unusual photos created by LEEROY Advertising Agency. New pictures added weekly.
Searchable: No
Attribution: Yes

MMT Stock (http://www.mmtstock.com/)
Beautiful collection of landscapes, etc. by Jeffrey Betts.
Searchable: Yes
Attribution: Check license

Morguefile (http://www.morguefile.com/)
Interesting images covering everything from animals to antiques.
Searchable: No
Attribution: Check license

New Old Stock (http://www.nos.twnsnd.co/)
Vintage photos from the public archives free of known copyright restrictions.
Searchable: No
Attribution: No

Picjumbo (http://www.picjumbo.com/)
They offer a free membership where you can download a few photos from each category, but to have full benefit of the site, you'll need a paid membership plan ranging from $10-$39 per month.
Searchable: No
Attribution: Check license

Pixabay (http://www.pixabay.com/)
Probably the number one choice for web designers. Easy to use search feature, and most don't require attribution.
Searchable: Yes
Attribution: Check license

Public Domain Archive
(http://www.publicdomainarchive.com/)
Breathtaking images. Just be sure you're in the "free" section because they also have a membership package at a reasonable price. $10 per month, I think.
Searchable: No

Ann Everett

Attribution: No

Snapwire Snaps
(http://www.snapwiresnaps.tumblr.com/)
7 free photos every 7 days.
Searchable: No
Attribution: Check license

Splitshire (http://www.splitshire.com/)
Beautiful stock photos.
Searchable: Somewhat
Attribution: Check license

Stockvault (http://www.stockvault.net/)
Over 20,000 photos to choose from.
Searchable: Yes
Attribution: Check license

Stokpic (http://www.stokpic.com)
10 new photos every 2 weeks.

Superfamous (http://www.superfamous.com/)
Super modern website showcasing the work of designer,
Folkert Gorter. It includes various collections of aerial,
biological, geological, and more.
Searchable: Somewhat
Attribution: Check license

Tookapic Stock
(http://www.stock.tookapic.com/?filter=free)
A marketplace where you can filter your choices by free
or premium (paid)

90

Searchable: Yes
Attribution: Check license

Unsplash (http://www.unsplash.com/)
Fabulous site! They add 10 royalty-free photos every 10 days. They even have a portfolio of how their images have been used by creative people.
Searchable: No
Attribution: Yes

Some Low-Cost Options
Even with the wide selection of free images from the above sites, you may not find the photo you have in mind. If not, then you may need to purchase one. Most sites offer monthly packages for those who use a lot of images or a per photo price for those who seldom need a picture.

I've listed only five sites, but there are more you can find by searching "stock photo sites."

Check each site to see current membership packages and price per picture cost.
http://www.adobestockphoto.com/
http://www.bigstockphoto.com/
http://www.dreamstimephoto.com/
http://www.fotolia.com/
http://www.istockphoto.com/

Again, check the license requirements before you download a "free" image to make sure you are using the photo within their guidelines.

Readers Judge a Book by its Cover

One of the biggest mistakes authors make is choosing the wrong cover art. Go to Amazon and look at the top selling books in your genre. How do the covers look? If you find one you like, then look inside the book and find the name of the cover designer. Once you know that, you can go to their website (many times there will be a clickable link shown) to see their portfolio and pricing.

Graphic designers have software with the ability to layer photos, shade, highlight, enrich the color, change colors of hair, eyes, clothing, add or remove tattoos, scars, and blemishes. In my experience, I've gotten covers done for both print and digital books from $60-$200.

The photo sites I've listed in the previous section will provide you with cover art, or your designer may have photos you can choose from. Sometimes, they do photography and design with exclusive images available.

Here are some designers I've used.

https://www.fiverr.com/rachelbostwick
http://www.pinkinkdesigns.com
http://www.artanddesignstudio.net
http://www.octagonlab.com/

Pre-made sites where you can purchase pre-designed covers and replace the title and author name to fit your book. Just keep in mind, the cover is bought "as is" except for changing the title and author name to yours. Prices vary.

https://www.facebook.com/search/top/?q=premades%204%20authors
http://www.creativeparamita.com/
http://www.premadebookcovers.com/
http://www.rockingbookcovers.com/
https://bookcovermachine.wordpress.com/
http://www.selfpubbookcovers.com/
http://paperandsage.com/site/
http://www.thecovercollection.com/premade-ebook-kindle-covers/authorgallery/

MARKETPLACE SITES

http://www.fiverr.com
http://www.guru.com

Fiverr and Guru are digital markets where you can get everything from a tarot reading to marketing services, starting at $5. I've had a few disappointing experiences on Fiverr, but for the most part, I've gotten nice results. I've had videos made. Formatting done. Book covers designed. Tarot readings for one of my characters. And a back cover summary.

When using a cover designer on Fiverr, I recommend you have an idea of what you want, and furnish the stock photos. Before placing an order, contact the vendor and let them know what you have in mind. Then they can furnish a quote. You'll pay more than $5, but much less than an individual designer fee. Keep in mind, vendors listed are from all over the world, and English may not be their native language, so make sure you can communicate with them before placing an order.

DIY COVER

If you have the nerve and patience, try your hand at designing your own cover. If you do, then CreateSpace has templates along with these sites:

http://www.bookdesigntemplates.com/ lovely templates compatible with many programs including MS Word. Prices range from about $50 and up.

http://www.coverdesignstudio.com has templates for covers that range from $19-$45. I've not used it, but it sounds easy. They also have interior templates.

http://www.diybookcovers.com teaches you how to do a cover in MS Word. Big learning curve with lots of patience needed.

If you try your hand at DIY design, keep this in mind:

Strong color contrast is best.

Red only looks good with black or white.

Use a color wheel for choosing colors.

Consider how the cover will look as a thumbnail.

White doesn't show up well unless you use a strong color with it.

Mix your fonts. Two is best, but no more than three — one fancy — the others plain.

Ann Everett

Here's a site where you can submit your cover for critique. The site owner gives a review, then commenters voice opinions. This is a good way to find out before you publish how your cover is received. They also have a list of designers.

http://www.covercritics.com

FORMATTING

Formatting your book into different files is a challenge. However, if you have patience, there are plenty of step-by-step instructions available.

If you publish both in print and digital, you will need several files.

PDF for print
ePub for KOBO, APPLE, & OTHER READERS
Mobi for Kindle

Most self-published authors use CreateSpace Print on Demand (POD) for their print books. CS has interior templates and a detailed guide for formatting. You can choose a blank template where you copy and paste your text into it, or a sample formatted template, where you remove the sample text and replace it with your own by directly typing into it.

The sample template contains formatted front matter, chapters, headers, page numbers, and more. To get started with either template, you have to choose the print size of your book, then download the corresponding template. I've listed the link along with others that are helpful.

How to create an interior PDF for your book.
https://www.createspace.com/Products/Book/InteriorPDF.jsp

A step-by-step guide to formatting your book's interior. https://www.forums.createspace.com/en/community/doc/DOC-1482

Interior templates. https://www.createspace.com/en/community/docs/DOC-1323

Get help with publishing your book. https://www.kdp.amazon.com/help?/topicId=A17W8UM0MMSQX6

You'll need an ISBN number which CS will provide for free, or you can purchase one from http://www.bowker.com/products/ISBN-US.html One number will cost about $125, or you can buy in quantity for a discount.

For the digital file, you must convert your word document. CreateSpace will do this for you, but I've never tried it. However, I have heard mixed reviews about using it.

If you do it yourself and then submit to KDP, there are instructions you can find online. I used *From Word Document to EBook,* by Ben Macklin. The download will cost you one dollar! It took some time to do the steps, but it worked, and KDP accepted the file.

The guide, with complimentary videos, can be purchased here: https://www.amazon.com/WORD-

EBOOK-guide-formatting-creating-
ebook/dp/B00900WP6S

It will take you through the process of stripping your Word document of formatting issues, adding styles, creating a table of contents, converting your Word document to an ePub and Mobi file using the free software Calibre and viewing your eBook on Adobe Digital Editions or Kindle Previewer. Before you strip the file, I suggest you make an additional copy of the entire manuscript to have on hand in case you need to start over from scratch. AND, always back your file up and on a thumb/flash drive.

With dozens of screenshots and plain English language, this step-by-step guide for people familiar with Microsoft Word and want to have a go at creating an eBook themselves.

When you upload to KDP, they will assign your digital file an ASIN number. There are also design and publishing tools you can use. The one I mentioned earlier, SCRIVENER is the most popular. There is a learning curve, but once you master it, I understand you'll love it! It costs about $50 for the program. You create a project file, and from that file, you're able to convert to digital and print books.
https://www.literatureandlatte.com/scrivener.php

Formatting For Hire

A good graphic designer will be able to "pretty" up your book interior because they use design software like In

Design, Photoshop, Gimp, etc. Not all graphic designers do formatting. Some stick to designing book covers. I'd look for one who does both because you usually get a price break if they do everything—print and digital interior files and covers.

Formatting for both print and digital can cost mucho $$ depending on how fancy you want them. I've listed sites below I've either used or have been recommended.

http://www.sherylleee.wixsite.com
http://www.pinkinkdesigns.com
http://www.artanddesignstudio.net
http://www.quantumformatting.weebly.com
http://www.integrityformatting.wixsite.com/integrity-formatting
http://www.fiverr.com
http://www.guru.com

DISTRIBUTION CHANNELS

These are channels you might consider to distribute your book.

CreateSpace—Amazon's Print on Demand (POD) division

Kindle Direct Publishing (KDP)—Amazon's digital (eBook) division

Draft2Digital—distributes multiple formats of your book, including ePub, Mobi, PDF, etc.

Be sure to read their terms, conditions, and tax information.

CATEGORIES

When you publish your book, you'll list it in categories. For my romance, Tell Me a Secret, the categories are:

Romance>New adult & college

Romance>contemporary

Romance>women's fiction

Make sure you get your book in the right category in the Kindle store because category affects recommendations. Do you ever get an Amazon email that says recommended for you? Well, the categories you search on Amazon tells them what you like, so from time to time, they'll recommend books to readers based on the category searches they've done.

SEO—SEARCH ENGINE OPTIMIZATION

What is a search engine?

Google, Bing, and Yahoo are the most popular.

What is SEO?

It is a combination of strategies and techniques used to get YOUR website/page/business/books, videos, etc. to show up on the first page of a search. And since most searchers don't look beyond the first three pages, you *need* to be on the first one. The search engine considers the most important listings and ranks them. The more you post, or the more visibility you have, the better chance you have of getting indexed on the first page.

So, when I google *Texas Romance Authors*, this is what comes up on that first page.

Texas authors of romance fiction
Welcome to North Texas Romance Writers of America
Heart of Texas Romance Authors

See how that works? Google picks up on those "keywords" in my search and gives me their best guess at what I'm looking for. Each listing has at least two of the words from my search.

KEYWORDS

So, let's talk about keywords and what they mean. It's pretty clear from the above example, how important they are. But how do I get Ann Everett to appear on that first page? Unless I join some of those keywords to my name, I won't be listed on the first page. However, if each time I blog, guest blog, promote on Twitter, Facebook, etc. I connect Texas Romance Author, Ann Everett, or #Texasromance #author Ann Everett. I may get there.

It may seem like overkill, but let's take my book, *Strong Verbs Strong Voice* as an example. If I write an article or blog about the book, then for maximum keyword usage, along with the word #verbs in the title, I should also have it on the title page, within the context of the article or blog, and in the URL stream.

Bottom line, keywords are words used as keys to unlock a search engine to find something specific, and the more places you use them, the more they will be connected to you.

On Amazon, they allow you to use up to seven keywords, but remember, phrases count as one word. I've also been told not to repeat your genre listing as keywords because Amazon automatically indexes those. If my book is contemporary romance, then I don't want to list those in my keyword choices. Instead, I may want to list elements included in the book. *Tarot card reader, Boho-chic fashion, motherhood, single mother, secrets, sex, happily ever after.*

Keywords + Ranking affects Amazon's Search Engine Optimization (SEO) which helps readers find your books!

Sales + Borrows affects your book's ranking on Amazon.

Anytime you can use keywords, do so.

MARKET

Sites and Tips

HARO—Help a Reporter Out

I suggest you subscribe to this site. You will receive an email three times each day filled with queries from magazine editors, TV producers, etc. Scroll through the requests and see if you fit any of the categories. If so, then answer the query with the information they require. You might end up on a television show or in a magazine article. There have been authors who hit the NYT Bestseller list after answering a HARO query, then getting booked on the Today Show. BAM! Two weeks later their book hit the top! I should mention it was a non-fiction book. But still, who knows? It could happen to you. Or better yet, me. LOL.

NEWSLETTERS

Most authors agree building a newsletter list is one of the best things you can do. Many successful authors swear their success is due to having a huge number of subscribers.

You can use a service like Mailchimp to keep track of your followers and automatically send your posts out to everyone at once.

http://www.mailchimp.com

A platform that shows you how to create email campaigns and landing pages to turn readers into subscribers. $29 per month up to 1000 subscribers.

http://www.convertkit.com

A great source for making your email fancy is WiseSTAMP. They have free and paid options.

http://www.wisestamp.com

This website tracks whether the emails sent by you were opened and read by the receiver. It also provides the recipient's IP Address, location, browser details, and more.
http://www.getnotify.com

STREET TEAM

I don't have a street team, not for the lack of trying, but so far no luck. I even have a name for my team if it ever happens. Sweet Thangs.

Anyway, a Street Team consists of fans/readers who agree to support your books as they are published, by tweeting, sharing on FB, blogging, reviewing, beta reading, etc. As a thank you, authors give those members advanced copies, and first notice of events, signings, special offers, sales, cover reveals, etc. Want to start one for me...or join one? Let me know!

SOCIAL MEDIA

First, let's talk about the different social media platforms and their benefits.

Facebook—Provides a good mix of friends and readers. Over one billion people login each day. Largest member age group is 35-54.

Twitter—The fastest place to find anything, and where readers can find you. According to http://www.paceco.com/insights/social-media/popular-social-media-demographics/ unlike FB, only 9% of Twitter users are between ages 50-64.

LinkedIn—Geared more to professionals, so finding and reaching editors, agents, etc., is easier.

Pinterest—Easiest to use and fun! Great for creating interest in your books by using visuals. Fastest growing social site.

YouTube—Where anybody can be a star! Brings your ideas to life and has the possibility of going viral!

Goodreads—Home to the largest group of readers in the universe, with groups in every genre known to man.

Google+—Biggest benefit here is getting your website indexed better by Google. The measurements below are required for setting up your profile.

Cover image—1080 X 608

Ann Everett

Profile photo—250 X 250

Image post—497 X 373

Instagram—Quickly becoming the social media choice among young people. If it's young readers you're looking for, then you should spend time on Instagram. They have over 400 million active users and more than half of those fall in the 18-29 age bracket.

If you like it or not, social media is mandatory for marketing. It is the fastest way to get traffic to your website, blog, or purchase links to your books. It allows you to connect with other authors in your genre. It provides the opportunity to share and promote your work by informing readers/followers about sales, contests, giveaways, cover reveals, and new releases.

AND, you get to do all that while sitting at your computer, wearing your pajamas!

Just keep in mind, building relationships, getting followers, and strengthening your platform, takes time.

Here are the pixel sizes to set up your profile page for Instagram.

Profile image— 110 X 110

Photo size— 1080 X 1080

Thumbnail photos— 161 X 161

Facebook

I once heard Facebook and Twitter compared to parties. Facebook is a family get-together where you know most everyone and there's plenty to talk about. Twitter is like a cocktail party where you spend a short amount of time meeting and greeting strangers.

According to everything I read, both are necessary but work in different ways. On average, Facebook members are older than those on Twitter. However, it's easy to set up a page on each site, and if you run into trouble, they both have help functions.

Those who can have pages on Facebook are businesses, organizations, individuals, and public figures. Only official representatives can create pages for organizations, businesses or public figures.

It's a place to share your story and connect with family and friends. Pages can be customized. People who "like" your page can get updates about you in their Newsfeed.

Members are welcome to have more than one page. Personal, business, even a page for each of your books. You should probably have a personal profile prior to setting up your business page.

To set up a Facebook page, go here.
http://www.facebook.com/pages/create

Once there, you'll choose page category, then select a more specific category from a drop-down menu, then choose "Artist, Band, or Public Figure.

The next drop-down menu should have an option for "author." Select it and then enter your author name.

Click "Get Started" and follow the series of steps. I think it's better if you answer each question, leaving none blank. Be sure and list your website URL along with any other social sites you use.

Include a picture or image for your profile keeping in mind this is the photo that will appear on every interaction you have on FB. The site has size restrictions so you may have to use a photo editing tool to reduce it down to a suitable size. Your word program should have one, but here are some you might try.

http://www.picmonkey.com
http://canva.com

The following sites are fun to use.
http://www.loonapix.com
http://www.bannersnack.com
http://www.rasterbator.net
http://www.screencast-o-matic.com

On all social sites, fill out the "About" section with as much info as you're willing to share. I'm told more is better.

After this, you'll need a cover image, also known as a banner. In this section, you should also have a "Call to

Action." Previously, I listed photo editing sites that have ready-made templates to use. If not, the measurements are listed below. If you can't do it yourself, there's no reason not to get a beautiful cover banner when you can use someone on Fiverr.com. You should be able to get one designed and formatted there for $5.

One advantage to a FB cover/banner is you can change it at any time to feature your latest release or whatever you choose.

Recommended sizes for **Facebook** are as follows:

Cover photo displayed on desktop browsers—828 X 315
For mobile 640 X 360
Profile photo 180 X 180
Images to post 1200 X 717

For examples of banners/headers take a look at some of your favorite authors FB pages. Here are a few examples I like.

https://www.facebook.com/LianeMoriartyAuthor/?hc_r
ef=SEARCH&fref=nf
https://www.facebook.com/DanielArenson/?hc_ref=SE
ARCH&fref=nf
https://www.facebook.com/NicholasSparks/

Don't expect Facebook to answer an inquiry. They have too many user/members to do that. However, they do have automatic responses when you report something posted that is against their guidelines, like nudity. You will receive notification when they act upon the report. Just be sure you get your account and page set up exactly the way you want, especially if you have more than one account/page. Because making changes is difficult once you have it in place.

Listed below are three author Facebook pages to provide inspiration.

Set up a "call to action" on your page. Choose wording like *Shop Now* or *Sign Up.* You can link your choice to your website or email newsletter subscriber form.

https://www.facebook.com/AuthorColleenHoover/
https://www.facebook.com/DebbieMacomberWorld/
https://www.facebook.com/MichaelConnellyBooks/

Okay, so you've got your page set-up, and the "Likes" are rolling in! To keep tabs on that growth, look above your banner. Listed there from left to right, you'll find these choices:

Page, messages, notifications, insights, publishing tools, settings, and help.

Click on insights, and you will be able to see the number of views, likes, engagements, reach, and actions you've had. You can look at the last seven days for an overview, or choose each section separately. Information provided will show the percentage of women and men fans you have along with their locations.

The graphs they provide help you determine if you're getting steady or sporadic growth. Peaks and valleys are typical, but the peaks will help you determine what promotion worked for you in getting people to "check you out."

Perhaps you did a guest blog on a certain date, and that caused an upward swing. Or maybe you held a paid campaign with a company like BookBub, and that caused a spike. If you ran an ad and got no increase, that will help you determine if you want to invest in that promotion again.

If your graph has flat-lined, then you need to make some changes. Post and promote more, either with FB ads or other promotional sites.

I suggest you click each button on the left-hand sidebar to see what they offer. You can even set up a shop on FB now and sell products!

You can invite people to "like" your page. You can "like" other people's pages, in hopes, they'll "like" you back. However, FB has guidelines if you solicit or "like" too many people in a short time, then FB will place you in "Facebook Jail." They'll cut you off for a while. Not sure about the time limit, but there is one.

They also limit the number of "likes" you can have. I think the number is 5,000. Social media changes all the time, so the rules you see this week may change without notice.

There is a "contact" section on FB, but like I said before, they don't answer individual inquiries. Their membership is too large, so don't look for answers there. Your best bet is to find something in their help section or search for answers on the web.

Here is the bad news about Facebook. On average, less than 20% of your fans see your posts. To reach 100%, you must purchase Facebook ads. If you do this, you can target the ad. If you're writing has been compared to Janet Evanovich, then target readers of her work.

Many authors use FB to grow their email lists by giving something away. Fund a FB ad to drive people to your website where they can sign-up for your email list and in return get a free download of whatever you're offering. Book, recipe, writing tips, etc.

Again, keep in mind, some will join to get the "freebie," then unsubscribe. Others won't open any newsletter email they get from you unless it has a catchy title. But you will get some sign ups who will love getting your newsletters as long as you don't flood their inbox!

I'm told the best time to post is Thursday, Friday, Saturday, and Sunday. The best times on average are 1-3 PM. Your Facebook insights will pinpoint when your followers/fans are using FB Go to Insights, then click Likes/Comments/Shares, then change to Engagement. This will show which of your posts are getting the most engagement.

Here are tools you may find helpful.

http://www.sumorank.com/fb-page/
http://likealyzer.com/
http://simplymeasured.com/free-social-media-tools
http://www.buzzsumo.com

Twitter

Unlike Facebook, Twitter doesn't prevent your followers from seeing your posts. You can also tweet as much as you like. No "Twitter Jail" for posting too much, too often. Twitter is also instant engagement. It's rapid-fire. However, if you try to follow too many people in a short amount of time, they may consider your requests spam. So, spread your requests out over a few days if you're doing a bunch.

To create a Twitter account, choose a "Twitter Handle," or you can use your profile name. Just make sure it's related to your author name or books.

Here, you'll also need a profile photo and header/banner.

Twitter Pixel Sizes

Header—1500 X 500 pixels

Profile photo—400 X 400

In-stream photos—440 X 220

Go here for help:
https://support.twitter.com/articles/127871

List your contact info, website URL, and a short bio.

Start following by using the Twitter search bar to find family, friends, fellow authors, enthusiastic readers, etc. Then start conversations. Just remember, the conversation can only be 140 characters, but use them all. Longer tweets are better.

Post interesting content. Ask questions. Join existing conversations. Be useful. Offer information. You can also promote your books, but I suggest you only promote free, special price offers, cover reveals, release day, positive reviews, etc. Don't be guilty of posting "buy my book, buy my book, buy my book." That will not get you followers.

One of the most important things is to be consistent in your posting whether it's once a day or once an hour. Use images in your posts. They attract much more attention. Especially if the photo is a cute animal!

Share the content from other people. By retweeting, your chances of getting the tweeter to follow you will increase. Share great blog articles. New releases from other authors. YouTube videos. Also, take quotes from a book by a well-known author and tweet those, giving the source. Perhaps the author themselves will retweet to all of their followers, thus giving your name out to them!

BE CAREFUL about what you post. Tone can't be heard in a tweet, so what sounds funny in your head, may come across as rude or even mean. A mistake like that can be a real "fan-killer." Social media is instant and public unless you have a private/protected profile. I always say, "Don't embarrass the family." If it's something you wouldn't say to your grandmother, then don't tweet it!

I just read where ALL CAPS and lots of !!!!!!!!!!! gets more attention. You may want to try that and see if the data is correct!!!!!!

Best Time to Tweet

Afternoon and closer to the weekend, especially Friday, Twitter traffic increases.

Now and then, it's okay to ask Tweeter and FB followers to retweet and share your posts. Maybe a sale or giveaway. Perhaps a charity event. It's okay to ask, just don't do it too much. However, if something is worth sharing, it's okay to tweet it several times. Just word it differently. Questions are always good to get attention and interaction. Make videos in connection with the release of your new book, and tweet questions.

Examples:

Which hunk would you choose to play ex-con, Rance Keller in Ann Everett's new release, Chirp? #badboy#Harleyrider#whiskeydrinker (this is 128 characters) Remember the limit is 140.

With the one above, I could post a photo of me holding two images of actors, marked A and B, who I think would be perfect for Rance.

In the one below, a photo or even a video of me making a peanut butter sandwich.

Do you spread peanut butter to the edge of bread like Blaze, from my new adult romance, Chirp? #awkward#PB&J#newadultromance (this is 125 characters)

I'd have my book shown as well. Those tweets encourage interaction, and I'm promoting my book without saying, **BUY MY BOOK!**

Tools to Help

There are tools to help you be more active on Twitter. You can use a service to schedule tweets, find people to follow, and keep track of who is talking about your tweets and topics related to your books and writing.

Tweetdeck is billed as the most powerful Twitter tool for real-time tracking, organizing, and engagement. Find everything they offer here: https://about.twitter.com/products/tweetdeck

With Hootsuite or Buffer, you can simplify and manage all your social media sites in one dashboard. Both free and paid plans are available. Find out their info here: https://hootsuite.com/products http://www.buffer.com

If you use a service to schedule posts for you, it's recommended you don't set the schedule up to auto-post everything. It's better to stagger the posts on all your social media. If you blog on Monday share it with Twitter. Then on Tuesday, share it with Facebook. Wednesday, LinkedIn. Thursday, Google+, etc.

You'll have some of the same followers on *all* social sites, so don't swamp them with the same posts on the same day. Spreading them over a week is best.

It's also better to divide your regular tweets (those other than a blog post) throughout the day. Maybe one every hour or two. That way, you'll reach more people and not clutter the Newsfeed of your followers. If you're in the middle of a conversation or doing a live event, then the "spread out" rule doesn't apply.

To establish a presence and get interaction, you should tweet at least five times a day. Two of those should be something of value. You can retweet informative articles, but it's a good idea to add a comment about the tweet instead of just retweeting.

Twitter Talk

So, what does all that Twitter talk mean?

#--Any word or phrase preceded by #. If you click on a hashtag, you'll see other tweets containing the same keyword or topic, like these.   #amwriting #amazon #funny #Texas

@--Used to bring attention to usernames in Tweets. People will use @username to mention someone or message or link to your profile.

♥ Click the heart under a tweet means you like it.

The single arrow is the reply button. Click it to respond to a tweet.

To retweet a tweet, click the two arrows

... For more options, click the three dots. Among your choices are: Share via Direct Message, Copy link to tweet, embed tweet, and report tweet.

Follow/unfollow

Click those to either add/request a follower or delete a follower. Remember, just because someone follows you doesn't mean you have to follow them back. If they sell a product you have no interest in, I recommend you don't follow. Chances are, they post numerous "ads," and you may not want your Newsfeed swamped with those.

Mention is when other users include the @ sign before a username.

Tweet button: This is a button you can add to your website which will allow you/users to include the link to their tweets.

SMS stands for Short Message Service, also known as text messaging.

DM stands for direct message. It is a private tweet that only the sender and recipient can read.

"Handle" refers to your user name.

Tweet- a post with a maximum length of 140 characters including URLs. Tweets are public to all, even people who aren't following you. If you don't already have it shortened, Twitter will do it for you.

Bitly

Bitly is the most popular URL shortening site and also provides data concerning the performance of those URLs. It's a good idea to get a shortened version of your book links and keep them in a document along with your longer URLs. That way, when you need either version, you'll have it available.
https://bitly.com/

Lists

With your Twitter account, you can create lists. That's a curated group of Twitter users you lump together and view tweet streams from only the people on that list. I think you can have twenty different lists.

They don't bring people to *your* tweets, only allows you to read tweets. However, the advantage is by grouping people, both followers and non-followers, you can manage your tweet reading. You can also subscribe to follow other people's lists. Say, writers in one, critiquers in another, libraries, agents, editors, formatters, designers, etc.

Remember, the lists are public, so don't give them a negative name like Dumb-butt agents to remind yourself of all the rejection letters you've gotten. Never know when one of those DBs might read and review your next book just to see if you've improved!

Popular television shows now conduct live tweet sessions either during the show or following an episode. This is a great way to interact with your favorite actors and actresses.

Twitter ads

Twitter offers advertising where you can target your tweets. I recently did a small paid ad with them, and even though the results report said it went out to over 3,000 people, I only received 7 clicks. I might have gotten a larger response for a bigger investment.

They track impressions and clicks. So even though thousands may see your ad, that won't always convert to clicks.

LinkedIn—This social media site may be underrated. According to Jorge Olson, best-selling business author, "Go to Facebook for likes, go to LinkedIn for sales." He says members here are 2X more likely to buy your book or product than FB, Google+, and Twitter combined!

Go here to read his interesting articles: http://www.linkedin.com/in/jorgeolson

Where most other social sites have more female users. More than half LinkedIn users are male. With more than 300 million users, the largest age demographic is 30-49.

A completed profile gets a better chance of appearing in searches.

The best way to market on LinkedIn is through blog posts with valuable content. You can add a WordPress app, so your blogs are shown. Such posts get thousands of views, which in turn will guide readers to your website to check out your books. You include your website URL to make it easy for them to head over there to find out more about you.

You can also link to Twitter, and your tweets will appear as status updates on LinkedIn.

Join groups and take part in discussions. Interaction is the best form of marketing on LinkedIn.

LinkedIn Pixel sizes

Background image—1500 X 425

Banner image—646 X 220

Standard logo—400 X 400

Profile photo—400 X 400

Career cover photo—974 X 330

Pinterest

For me, unlike all the other social media sites, Pinterest is addictive! They should have named it, that's so cute! Because once I look at all those pins, that's what I say. "Oh, that's so cute! Look, that's so cute!"

The first thing you want to do on Pinterest is sign up for a business account. That way, you'll have access to analytics, and your website will get verified. Once that's done, the images you post will have a better chance of getting search results.

Use your author name as your username because that helps brand you, so use it as it appears on your books.

Just like every other site, you'll enter a profile, headshot, keywords, etc.

Profile photo—165 X 165

Board display—22 X 150

Pin sizes—236 pixels wide

You'll also want to add an icon Pinterest button to your website, so visitors can check out your boards by clicking the icon and going directly to your Pinterest page.

Not a good idea to connect your Pinterest account to any other social sites. If it automatically posts on Twitter, the pin will only be a link and not an actual photo.

You'll want to add a Pinterest bookmark to your browser, and you can find those instructions here: http://www.pinterest.com/about/goodies

On Pinterest, you can follow pinners (members) or their individual boards. Now, about those boards. Maybe you love jewelry or fashion or cars or like me, everything Texas. You can make boards for all your favorites, but don't forget to make a board for each of your books! More on that later.

Look at other pinners, even authors, to get ideas of what they pin.

You can use the search bar on Pinterest to find items/images. Once found, you can pin directly from the web, or if you have personal images on your desktop, you can pin those. When you pin a personal image, be sure and include your website URL in the description/comment section.

By clicking the Pinterest logo at the top of your Pinterest page, you can navigate to the Newsfeed and find everything pinned by people you follow. Click Analytics and discover how many of your pins are getting RE-pinned.

Board Ideas

Here are the boards I have related to my books.

A board for each book with fantasy cast, quotes, covers, etc.

Images of wedding dresses

A collection of jewelry

One of my characters loved Boho-chic, so I have a board for that.

Beautiful Men

Beautiful women

Quotes that will make you laugh

Recipes from my Sweet Thangs Cookbook

Books I love

Boots and hats

All things Texas

DIY

As you can see, your boards should be all about what you like. Go crazy! You can even have secret boards. Why? Well, if you're a Stuart Reardon fan, like me, and have a hard time finding a photo of him suitable for public viewing, a secret board is a good thing!!

Here's a fun site to make beautiful posts for social media. They have 1000's of templates.

http://easil.com

YouTube

Even if you don't make videos, you can post a book trailer on YouTube. Today, with iPhones, you don't need any special equipment, so it's never been easier. All you need is an idea, but even if you don't want to post videos, there are other ways to use YouTube.

You can share a video.

Connect with book vloggers.

And, I'm sure you know how valuable YouTube is for research. Want to know how to do a PowerPoint presentation, embed a video on YouTube, and find travel locations for your next book? There are YouTube videos for all that.

If you do your own, keep a few things in mind.

Videos should be short.

Longer ones need to be divided up into segments.

Use keywords in your description.

Make sure the lighting is good.

Ann Everett

You can even start your own channel.

And as with all social sites, sharing, commenting, liking, and following plays a big part in connecting with others.

Size for Video uploads—1280 X 760

Channel cover photo—2560 X 1440

YouTube Ideas:

Your book release or cover reveal

A book signing event or conference

Offer writing or editing advice

Prepare and share a quick recipe that one of your characters loves to make

OR, if you have a cookbook, prepare and share a recipe from it

Answer questions from readers

Maybe you had a marketing campaign that went well, share the results.

Let someone interview you on camera.

Build a playlist of songs you'd use if your book was made into a movie.

Goodreads

It's important to list your books on Goodreads because it has the world's most dedicated readers and reviewers.

128

Over 55,000,000 of them. But be prepared, the reviews you get there, on average, will be more critical than those on Amazon. Here's what you need to do.

Set up an account.

Set up an author profile. You'll need a picture and a bio.

Add all of YOUR books to the site.

1. Sign in or sign up.
2. Search for your author name to find your books. If your books aren't there, then add them manually. If they are there, proceed to number three.
3. Click on your name located below the book title.
4. Scroll to the bottom of the page and click…"is that you?" This will send a request to join the Author Program. It may take a few days to process your request. When it does, you'll receive an email confirmation along with instructions on how to manage your author profile.

You can also create a fan page public group.

Add books you've read.

Write reviews.

Rate books. Participate in Q&A events concerning your books and those written by other authors.

Sync your blog to Goodreads, that way when you post a blog, it will automatically post to Goodreads on your profile page. This will help guide readers to your website.

1. Go to your author profile; http://www.goodreads.com/author/show
2. Scroll down and click on your blog, then on the right side of the page, blog settings.
3. Look for something that says, add URL or add an external feed URL.
4. Paste in your RSS feed into the box and click, "add feed."
5. You'll be directed to a page asking if this is your blog. If the URL is correct, check "yes."
6. If asked, answer "save" your previous blog posts. They should integrate into your feed.
7. Go to your Goodreads page to check your blog. It should be there.

You also have an events section where you can share your upcoming book signings and speaking engagements.

Add your books to **Listopia**, found on the explore menu. Find examples here: https://www.goodreads.com/list

This is a free tool where you can list your own books and books by other authors. It works in your favor to list books of similar writers' right along with yours. You can add to existing lists or create your own.

1. Click "Create a list" on the top right-hand corner of the page.

2. Sign in or sign up to create a Listopia account.

3. Click Explore, and choose Listopia from the drop-down menu.

4. Click "Create a List."

5. Fill in the requested information which will consist of:

The title of Your List. Make it searchable by book titles, keywords, other best-selling authors' names.

Description. This should be a summary of what your list contains.

Tags. Use keywords that will help readers find your list.

Add Books. Yours and other authors. You can add from Goodreads or Amazon.

6. Then click preview to review your list. Once satisfied, click publish.

Share excerpts from your books.

Post videos or book trailers.

Add a Goodreads author widget to your website or blog.

Do a book giveaway.

Remember to choose if you want the giveaway to include foreign countries or just the US. Take into consideration Goodreads only allows print copies for giveaways, and out of country postage is very expensive, costing anywhere from $20-$60 per book.

Goodreads furnishes author support through their tutorial page and Author Help section.

REVIEWS

Reviews help to drive sales.

Professional review sites Amazon accepts:

http://www.kirkus.com
http://midwestbookreview.com/get_rev.htm
http://www.blueinkreview.com

Some of these professional sites charge for reviews, some don't. However, if they accept donations, I recommend you give one, especially if they give your book a nice review!!

If I ever figure out the secret to getting guaranteed reviews and plenty of them, I'll sell that secret and become a Gazillionaire! I don't have a clue how to get hundreds of reviews. Lord knows I've tried just about every way and here's the weird thing. I have two best-selling books that have sold thousands, and they still have less than a hundred reviews!

I've checked my favorite author's books which are both NYT and USA bestsellers, and many of their books have few reviews. I read that for every 5,000 books you sell, you may get 5 reviews if you're lucky. Because of my personal experience, I believe that.

Some places sell review services, and maybe they work, but the problem is, if Amazon finds out you've paid a service, they'll remove the reviews! Even now, I'm hearing reviews gotten via blog tours are sometimes disappearing. There are guidelines they can follow to be legitimate. Just make sure the service/blog tour you use is within those guidelines.

However, let me offer all the ways you can try to get reviews.

Start before your book releases!!!! This is most important! Sending ARC's (Advanced Reading Copies) is the best way to get reviews early. I'd recommend 6-8 weeks prior to release. I know that's hard because you have your book done and you're just dying to get it out for the world to see. But you must exercise patience!

***Again, keep in mind, Amazon has changed the acceptable wording for reviews posted from those who received and ARC. They must now include in their review:

I received an Advanced Reading/free copy of this book in consideration of a voluntary review. I have voluntarily reviewed this book.

Here is a service you might consider for sending Advanced Reading Copies or any free files you offer. They charge a small yearly fee. At this printing, I think it's about $20 per year. Well worth it if you're offering something free to build your email list. That can run into hundreds of downloads for multiple readers.

http://www.bookfunnel.com/

BLOG TOURS

This is another reason for the 6-8 week waiting period before release. Most tour companies book at least 6 weeks out. That is if you want a Release Day Tour. You can book a tour after your book comes out, but again, plan early if you want a particular date.

A Release Day Tour will get you reviews as I mentioned earlier. Here's how it works. You pay a fee to the tour blogger (hopefully a blogger with a huge following), and in return, she gets other bloggers to consider reading and posting a review of your book on Amazon and Goodreads. Some may only post on their personal blogs and Amazon.

Since all bloggers have followers, if they choose to review your book, lots of readers should see it, and hopefully result in sales and more reviews.

The tour company handles everything. You send them a digital copy, and they distribute it to the bloggers who sign up for the tour. Keep in mind, you are furnishing them with an ARC (Advanced Reading Copy) in consideration of a review and not every blogger will like your book! However, the tour company generally asks participants NOT to post a review that is less than 3 stars, until after the book has been out for a few weeks. You may still get a number of less than wonderful reviews, but at least they won't appear on your release day.

You will receive a copy of all sites taking part in the tour, and you should go to each one and thank the blogger and if you have comments there, thank those commenters, too.

Here are top blog tour sites that offer a variety of packages.

http://www.xpressobooktours.com
They have over 6,000 Goodreads Followers, and an average of 34,000 page views on their blog each month. I've used this service and recommend it.

http://www.bookenthusiastpromotions.com
A site that offers many services and accepts different genres. I've used this service and recommend it.

http://www.enchantedbookpromotions.com
They've hosted over 800 tours. Packages start as low as $35.00.

http://www.bewitchingbooktours.com
This site is open to all genres but specializes in paranormal romance and urban fantasy.

http://www.goddessfish.com/
Although their site is not as user-friendly as some, they have hosted more than 2,000 tours. I have used them and recommend their service. Packages start at $55.

http://www.rockstarbooktours.com/
This site does promotions for FREE. They specialize in YA books, but I think they may accept other genres.

Because it's free, they book months in advance, so start early to get a date scheduled.

http://yaboundbooktours.blogspot.com/p/services.html
Another YOUNG ADULT site. Packages start at %50.

You can find other tour companies by searching for "book tour companies" or adding your genre, "best (your genre) book tour companies."

Be sure and read their submission guidelines and look for testimonials.

OR, you can find and solicit bloggers to review your book on your own. Where?

Twitter—It's easy to use their search bar to identify readers of your genre. Type in the search bar, "(your genre) book blogger." This will get you a list of those fitting that criteria. Above the first listing on the right, click "view all" and more will come up. Click on each one to see how many followers they have and if the blogger is active in reviewing books. If they haven't posted/tweeted much recently, or have few followers, it's not worth your time to contact them.

From their listing, you can find their website which will have submission guidelines for submitting a book for review. If your book doesn't fit their guidelines, then don't submit it!

Go to **Amazon** and **Goodreads** and look at authors who write similar to you and reach out to reviewers who have reviewed them. If the reviewer has a contact email or website listed, use that, if not, then on Goodreads there is a feature where you can "send a message" to members. Ask them kindly if they will read and review your book.

Many times you can do a review swap. I'll read yours if you read mine. Again, there are groups on Goodreads where you can do this.

Ask friends, family members, people you work with, church friends, even friends from high school and college, etc. to read and post a review. Go to your email list and FB followers, then contact them with the request. Be sure and make a list of who you've asked and their response and when you sent the digital file to each person.

You should include directions on how to open Mobi, ePub, or PDF. If they have a Kindle or Nook, they should have a Kindle or Nook email address, and you can send the appropriate file directly to their digital reader.

If you have some who only read print copies, then plan to provide those. Remember, you can order print proof copies without the book being published. Also, give them a deadline to post a review. Keep in mind, not everyone will review the book even if they say they will!

A simple email request is all you need. I'll use my name as an example. In the subject line, I'll say, Ann Everett's New Book or Ann Everett's Newest Book or The Last Book in Ann Everett's (name of the series) Series, or The Second Book in Ann Everett's (name of series) Series!

Hi (Name),

Soon, I will release my latest book, (title), and because your opinion is important to me, and reviews are essential to Indie Authors, I hope you'll help me.

I'd love to send you a free advance copy of my book. All I ask is that you consider reviewing the book, and if you choose to do so, then post a review on Amazon, Goodreads, or both.

I have digital copies available. Just let me know which type of file you need.

I look forward to hearing from you.

Thanks so much,

(Your Name)

For those who agree, send the book quickly. You should have Mobi, ePub, and PDF files to choose from. You may also want to provide instructions on how to download each of those files onto their device. Those directions can be found on the internet.

It's a good idea to keep a list of those you asked and those who agreed. That way, you can keep account of who should be posting reviews.

Then, ten days before release, check in with those who agreed to read, review, and post on release day. This is just a nice way to remind them.

Subject line: Only XX days until the release of (Title) on XX/XX/20XX!

Title and release day listed in the subject line serves as a quick reminder. Then repeat it again in the email body.

Hi (name),

Thanks again for considering to review (TITLE)!

In ten more days, on XX/XX/20XX, I'll hit that publish button and put it out there for the world! I'm excited you have been one of the first I've shared my story with, and your thoughts about the book mean everything to me.

If you're not sure about where to leave the review, no worries. I'll send you a link when it's time to post!

Keep in mind your review doesn't have to be long and detailed. It can be as simple as a couple of sentences of what you liked about the book. Also, it is required by Amazon and Goodreads that you state within your review: I received a free copy of this book in consideration of a voluntary review.

Have a wonderful day!

(Your Name)

Then, on launch day, send one final email with the review link.

The easiest way to do this is to use MailChimp if you're doing a lot. You can schedule an email with this service to go out the morning of release to all those who agreed to post a review on release day. It will give them one last nudge to get it done!!

http://www.mailchimp.com/

Subject line: YAY!!! Release Day of (Title) is finally here!!!

Hi (Name),

One last reminder that today my new book, (Title) releases and if you chose to review, you can now post it!!

Thank you from the bottom of my heart for helping get (Title) off to a great start. Here is a link to Amazon and Goodreads. Click each link, and it will take you to the place to post your review.

Amazon<<<list link here.

Goodreads<<<list link here.

Thanks again for helping me with this. I am blessed to have a friend like you!

(Your Name)

Then, after your book has been out for a week to ten days, send a note of thanks to those who posted a review even if they didn't do it on release day. You should have already thanked them on the site where they posted.

You might also offer something for free, like recipes, or a short story. It's an excellent opportunity to send each reviewer a small "Thank you" gift. You can do this via an attachment to the email.

Sites for finding reviewer/bloggers

The Book blogger List http://www.bookbloggerlist.com
This site has a list of bloggers organized by genre. Some offer tours.

Kate Tilton's Book Bloggers
http://www.katetilton.com/kate-tiltons-book-bloggers/
Another site with a list of book bloggers who will review indie authors.

Story Cartel https://www.storycartel.com
On this site, authors can submit their books for free in consideration for honest reviews from readers.

The Indie View http://www.theindieview.com/indie-reviewers
Huge listing of indie book reviewers.

The YA Book Blog Directory
http://www.yaboookblogdirectory.blogspot.ca
This directory focuses on Young Adult books only and has a large listing of YA book review bloggers.

Always respond to 3-5 star reviews you get on Amazon and Goodreads. Readers took the time to read and review your book, so the least you can do is thank them. Even if the review is less than glowing, NEVER engage the reader by defending your work. Some readers are looking for a fight because they thrive on that sort of thing. This is what I write when the reviewer gives me a 3-star negative review.

Hi (Name)

Thank you so much for reading (book title), and taking the time to leave a review here. It means the world to me. ~~Ann

Now, should a reader contact you with negative things to say about your book, which they can do through your website contact, do not be snarky. EVER. One unhappy reader can do you real damage. They can copy and paste anything you write and put it all on FB and Twitter, and any other place they want. So, mind your manners.

It is far better to say…Thank you for contacting me. I plan to update this story soon and will consider your excellent suggestions.

Goodreads recommends you NOT reply to less than three-star reviews, and I don't. I also follow that same rule on Amazon.

One way to move a 1-star review down on your Amazon book page is to click that the review wasn't helpful. Get friends to do the same, and that review will be replaced by one not as bad. Your book page will still show the most negative and positive reviews at the top, but that little trick will help move that scathing review out of first place and replace it with one less offensive.

Always remember, not everyone will love your book, and that's okay. Even the Bible has plenty of less than 5-star reviews. One person's opinion of your book is not the end of the world. Suck it up and go on with life.

LAUNCH PARTY

The difference between a release blog tour and launch party is simple. The blog tour is virtual, and a launch party is physical. A "birth" day party for your book. So, you'll treat it like a party with invitations, decorations, refreshments, etc.

Concentrate on FARPS. Yeah, say that fast three times, and it comes out stinky.

Festive— Find or design a festive location that connects to your book. In my Tizzy/Ridge Trilogy, many scenes take place in Sweet Thangs Bakery. I had a successful book signing at a local cooking school! They prepared recipes from the companion cookbook I published, Sweet Thangs—Southern Sweets from Two Sassy Sisters.

It isn't necessary to match a setting from your book. It can be at your home or a friend's house who has a large dining or pool area. In my new adult romance, Tell Me a Secret, Maggie loves the gazebo in her backyard. Our local park has one which provided a free location!

Atmosphere—Don't line chairs around the room. Make the party memorable. Arrange group seating. In my contemporary romance, Say You'll Never Love me, the main character, Raynebeaux Starr, reads tarot cards. Having a fortune teller at my launch party was so much fun!

Raynebeaux also has a certain fashion style. Boho-chic. A great way to build on the atmosphere was to have a dressing station set up where guests could put on fringed vests, wild jewelry, tie crazy scarves around their heads, then take photos, then post them on social media!

In my Tizzy/Ridge Trilogy, Jinx, the bartender, makes several signature drinks. We used some of those recipes for refreshments. The more things you can tie your book to, the better!

I create fantasy casts for all my books and make storyboards. I set up a voting booth for guests to cast their ballot for the one they liked the most.

Reviews—Why not have your laptop set up for attendees to post reviews? Or even better, have them bring their own laptop and use it to post. No question some of them read an ARC or perhaps they belong to your critique group where you read chapters. This is the perfect time to boost reviews, so take advantage of it!

At some point in the evening, you'll be expected to speak. If you read from your book, don't do more than 2-3 pages. There is nothing more boring than listening to someone read, unless you're in a coma, and then I hear it's a good thing!!

Choose a funny scene if you have one and post on social media. If not, then one with an animal or child in it!!

Those are always popular!! If it's a non-fiction book, then choose a helpful passage.

Prizes—Nothing makes party goers happier than to win prizes or leave with swag! In my latest book, Chirp, one of my characters makes goats milk soap. The story is set in the imaginary town of Bluebird, Texas, home of the Bluebird Festival. I mention in the story they have tee-shirts that read, Come Fly With Me to Bluebird, Texas. I plan to give away several gift baskets with a tee-shirt, soap, bookmark, and a signed book. I'll also give bluebird houses as prizes…which my husband can build for practically no cost!

Here are sites to help with party games.

Here, you can make a word search containing words from your book. Whoever solves the puzzle first, wins!

http://puzzlemaker.discoveryeducation.com/WordSear chSetupForm.asp?campaign=flyout_teachers_puzzle_w ordcross

This is a great site for all sorts of quizzes.

http://www.playbuzz.com/

These two sites allow you to make a puzzle from your own photo. Once done, you'll get a URL to your creation you can use online. Think of using your cover or characters from your book.

http://www.jigzone.com/

http://www.jigsawplanet.com/

Sales—Nothing makes an author happier than to sell books!! So, make it easy. Reduce the price of your print copies for the party. Why not have all your books at a special party price? You cover the tax. Have plenty of cash for change and if you don't have Square, then get one, so you'll be able to accept credit and debit cards. Make sure your books are displayed in more than one place. That way, your guests can look without standing in line. You want to make buying easy!

What is Square? It's a card reader that plugs into your iPhone and allows you to accept payment just like a regular credit card machine. You can set it up, so the deposits go directly to your bank account, savings account, or PayPal account. Cost begins at $29 for a basic chip reader Square. You are charged a small fee each time it's used which is deducted from the amount of deposit. You must get one. Hardly anybody carries cash or checks anymore!

https://squareup.com/shop/hardware

Be sure and have a signing area with a good pen. I sign all my books in pink ink. If you do something similar, then make sure you have plenty of those special pens on hand.

How much will all this cost? Once you get friends to help host the party, chances are they will contribute. By pooling resources, you can throw a shindig on a budget. Your biggest expense will be prizes and party favors, but you can control that. Set a budget and stick with it. Think of it as an investment in getting your book off to a good start.

AMAZON MARKETING OPPORTUNITIES

Amazon will walk you through the set up for each campaign, and if you have questions, they get back to you quickly with an answer.

Go to your KDP Bookshelf. To the right of each book, in a rectangular box, you'll see Promote and Advertise. Click that, and your choices will come up.

Kindle Countdown Deal

This allows you to run a limited-time discount promotion for your book. The special price will appear along with the regular price on the book's detail page. It will also have a clock showing how much longer the special price will be in effect. As a member of KDP Select, you will still earn the higher royalty during the Countdown Deal.

If you have a series, running the first book at a reduced price will most times drive sales for the other books in that series. It will also get you reviews and raise your ranking during that promotion.

There are rules:

Your book must have been enrolled in Kindle Select for 30 days and have not changed the price for 30 days or more before you can run a Countdown Deal.

The minimum discount off regular price is $1 U.S. and 1 pound UK.

Latest end date of your countdown must be 14 days before your Kindle Select contract expires. However, if you renew the Kindle Select program, then the end date for your countdown can be the last day of your current program expiration.

Check Kindle's information for all the rules, because they may change.

Free Book Promotions

Out of each 90-day contract with KDP, authors can offer any book in the program for free, for up to 5 days. Since the book will be free, you will not make any royalties from those downloads. However, the free offering will get readers to your page and perhaps increase sales of your other books and also raise ranking and garner reviews.

Countdown Deals and Free Promotions can be scheduled for several books at a time if you choose and are cost free to you.

There are also book promotion sites that will promote your book at no cost. However, these generally have to be scheduled early, so consider that when planning a promotion.

AD Campaign

This is a pay per click promotion where you set the budget of what you wish to spend each time a customer clicks on your book. NOT buys your book, but clicks on your book.

You choose how long you want the ad to run.

To qualify for this program, your book must be available on Amazon.com, be published in eBook format with KDP, written in English, and meets Kindle's Acceptance Policies.

You can promote either by Sponsored Product ads which involve using keywords, or Product Display ad, which is genre targeted.

Once you choose the type of campaign, then you'll select your targeting.

Automatic—targets your ad to all relevant customer searches based on your product information.

Manual—add your own keywords or phrases to your campaign.

Product Display Ad—target your ads by related products (other books, or by customer interest.) These ads may appear on Kindle E-reader screens.

For the full information and rules of these programs, go to your book page and click on the choices offered.

Amazon Giveaway

This can be found on your Amazon author book page. Click on any of your books, then scroll down past the reviews and you'll see, "set up a giveaway." Amazon will walk you through the procedure. Since you're giving the book away, you'll get no royalties, so what is the advantage?

Followers: You can require contestants to follow your author page on Amazon. All those followers get a notice each time you have a new book released. Amazon does that work for you, and it will help your book get off to a good start.

Traffic: According to Amazon, Giveaways increase traffic to your books more than 40% during the promotion.

Twitter Exposure: If you tweet #AmazonGiveaway, everyone searching for Amazon Giveaways will see that tweet…and you!

Minimal investment: The only cost you have is the cost of your book. You chose how many you want to giveaway, so you control the investment. I've done one book per fifty followers and gave away five books. That netted me 250 followers with each giveaway. Keep in mind, you will make a royalty off each book because you've purchased them at regular price, so that reduces your cost.

Audience: Readers who love romance will search for romance giveaways, therefore targeting the exact reader

I'm looking for. It's the same with each genre, so this fine-tunes your followers.

You can run a giveaway and a Kindle Countdown at the same time for the same book. If you do that, then your cost will be less because you're not paying the full price for the giveaway book, AND you're making the higher royalty because it's in KDP Select.

PROMOTION SITES

I could list hundreds of sites available for promotion. Many will promote your "special or reduced" price book for free, and some will charge. Some offer both. A free section, and a fee-based section. Only the fee-based will guarantee your book will be featured on their site.

The more popular sites, like, BookBub, Robin Reads and Ereader News Today (ENT), book weeks in advance, so you need to contact them early.

You will also need to *subscribe* to their mailing list, so you'll receive the post of your book on the day they advertise it. It will not appear on their site...only in the newsletter, they send out.

http://www.armadilloebooks.com
http://www.awesomegang.com
http://www.bargainebookhunter.com
http://www.bestebookfree.com
http://www.bookangel.co.uk.com
http://www.bookasaurus.com

http://www.bookgorilla.com
http://www.bookrhythm.com
http://www.booksbutterfly.com
http://www.bookdealsdaily.com
http://www.booksgosocial.com
http://www.booksgoodies.com
http://www.bookloversheaven.com
http://www.bookpinning.com
http://www.bookscream.com
http://www.booksontheknob.com
http://www.bookzio.com
http://www.buckbooks.com
http://www.clickreading.com
http://www.contentmo.com
http://www.dailycheapreads.com
http://www.digitalbooktoday.com
http://www.ebookshabit.com
http://www.ebooklister.com
http://www.ereaderutopia.com
http://www.ereadercafe.com
http://www.free99books.com
http://www.freebie4mom.com
http://www.freebooks.com
http://www.freebooksandmore.com
http://www.freebooksblog.com
http://www.freebookclub.org
http://www.freebookdude.com
http://www.freedigitalreads.com
http://www.frugal-freebies.com
http://www.thefussylibrarian.com
http://www.indiebookoftheday.com

http://www.inspiredreads.com
http://www.thekindlebookreview.com
http://www.kornerkonnection.com
http://www.pixelscroll.com
http://www.promocave.com
http://www.readingdeals.com
http://www.readfree.ly/
http://www.readingdeals.com
http://www.readinghud.com
http://www.romancebookdeals.com
http://www.sweetfreebooks.com
http://www.thereadingsofa.com
http://www.yourdailyebooks.com

As with everything on the internet, sites come and go. Some of these may no longer be available.

PAID ADVERTISING

As and author, I get emails all the time offering fantastic results for getting reviews, sales, more FB followers, Twitter followers, etc. All I have to do is pay a fee or a monthly membership. In the beginning, I bought into some of those and spent money I wish I had back. This is what I learned. Before investing, check out the authors who have endorsed the company. How high are their books ranked on Amazon? How many reviews do they have? When I google them, how much is listed about them?

If they only have a few reviews and rankings no higher than mine, then I delete the offer.

Google AdWords

I have not used Google AdWords, but have an author friend who did. He used a $10 per day budget, which meant his "bid" per click ran $1-$2 and landed him between the 2nd and 4th page of the search. He got no sales from this campaign. However, he saw a slight increase in visits to his website.

If you try one, he recommends calling Support @ 1-866-246-6453 and have them walk you through the process because it's complicated, and a mistake can cost you $$.

https://www.google.com/adwords/

Goodreads Ads

While Goodreads boasts more than 300 million page views and over 40 million unique visitors each month, my research suggests that authors get more from doing a Goodreads Giveaway than running an ad campaign.

I have not done paid advertising with Goodreads, but I know it is also a "per click" program where you control the budget and length of the campaign.

Find out all about it here:
https://www.goodreads.com/advertisers

Amazon Affiliate Program

Amazon's affiliate program is where you affiliate your website with other sellers by listing their ads. If someone clicks that ad from your site and makes a purchase, then you get paid a percentage. Sometimes, as high as 15%. The link below is recent as of this writing and has useful information.

http://www.shoutmeloud.com/how-to-make-money-with-amazon-affiliate-progrram.html

Sidebar Advertising

This is where you pay to have your book listed on the outer border of a (blogger, tour company, etc.) website. I did this with a blogger who had a gazillion visitors to her site each month. She also had a large following of readers. As far as I know, I didn't sell a single book from my thirty-day ad.

There may be other authors who have done well with this type of ad, but I did not.

Online Magazine Ads

I've also tried online magazine ads with two different publications. Neither proved beneficial.

Most social media sites now offer paid advertising opportunities. I won't go into all those because you can go to each site and get all the information. However, I will talk about examples of free advertising/promotion you might consider to engage readers. Most of your interaction will probably come from Facebook, but you can adjust these suggestions to use on other social sites.

1. Ask fans a question or for their opinion about something concerning your book.

Fans love to interact and speak with authors, so starting a conversation is a great way to get a buzz going about your book.

2. Give fans the opportunity to ask YOU a question.

Facebook parties are perfect for this. Some companies can set one up for you, or you can do it yourself. However, be prepared for rapid fire questions. Typically, you schedule a time and send invitations to your followers. If you give a prize or two, even better. That encourages people to attend.

3. Share quotes from your books.

I've done this on Twitter and Facebook. Be sure and use an image when you post quotes because they get a lot more attention.

4. Post photos of your pets

Post photos of the fictional pets from your books. Animals and babies get the most response on social sites like FB and Twitter and Pinterest!

5. Do a cover reveal.

You can coax people to your website to find out more about the book and characters. While there, they can sign up for your newsletter, and receive a free gift, which can be a short story, recipes, free book, etc.

6. Share character interests.

Maybe you have a character with a shoe or jewelry fetish. Post photos of those. You might even put on a pair and take pictures of just your feet in stilettos! Sexy photos stir up lots of conversation.

7. Share your workspace.

Fans are interested in seeing where you work. Messy? Neat? I keep a dry erase board on the back of my door and make notes as I think of them. Maybe you have a storyboard with all the props and characters in your books. Like a hard copy of a Pinterest board! Posting photos of anything work related is a good way to connect with readers.

8. Book events

Post photos of events you've done. Book signings. Career Expos. Speaking engagements. Charity/volunteer work. These are always great opportunities to donate books.

9. Hold a contest

Ask readers to name a character or suggest a title for your book. Have a bakery in your story? Antique cars? Dog parade? Ask readers to share one of theirs. What about asking readers to take a photo of your cover in crazy places and send it to you? For any contest, you'll want to award a prize, and it can be anything from free autographed books to nightshirts!

10. Share links and websites.

As an example: Maybe you have a series with veterinarians. If you find interesting websites or links discussing animal illnesses, tips, funny videos, etc., share those.

11. Celebrate a character's birthday or anniversary.

Maybe they aren't real, but hey, everyone likes a party. Have readers send their idea of what to serve at the celebration. If they send photos, even better!

12. Create a game

The sites below are educational sites, but you can use them to create puzzles that pertain to your books. I've created word find puzzles for all of my books. Other than posting online, they're great fun to take when you speak to small groups or book clubs.

https://learningcanbefun.wikispaces.com/QuizCreators
https://www.discoveryeducation.com/free-puzzlemaker/

PINTEREST

You can "promote" pins on Pinterest, which is another pay per click campaign. Go to the two sites below for complete information.

https://help.pinterest.com/en/articles/creating-and-editing-promoted-pins
https://business.pinterest.com/sites/business/files/pinterest-ads-manager-guide.pdf

RECOMMENDED SITES

Marketing Advice and Information

http://www.enovelauthorsatwork.com
http://www.indiesunlimited.com
http://wwpreditorsandeditors.com

Promote your books for free or for a fee, go to the sites below. I've used many of these places. Choosy Bookworm, Digital Book today, Ereader News today (ENT), Indies Unlimited, Awesome Gang, and others.
http://www.authorreach.com
https://www.kindlepreneur.com/list-sites-promote-free-amazon-books/

An article of 100 + places to market your romance/erotica books.
http://marketingforwriters.com/100-places-to-market-your-romanceerotica-book/

BookBub~~GAME CHANGER

Not only is it difficult to get accepted by BookBub, but it will also cost you a lot of money to do an ad with them. However, out of all the advertising/marketing I've done, I've gotten the best results there.

I've been rejected more times than accepted. That's the typical outcome for most authors I know. Here I will share the first ad I did with them.

I submitted the second book in my Tizzy/Ridge Trilogy, *You're Busting My Nuptials,* as a mystery, and offered it for free.

They accepted the book but changed the genre from mystery to chick lit. Which worked since half of the story involved three women characters. That saved me some bucks because the mystery ad would have cost over two hundred and the chick lit ad cost seventy.

Remember, this was to offer my book for free! I wouldn't make a dime off a single download. However, the other two books in the series were regular price, so I hoped to sell some of those. Fingers, eyes, legs crossed.

Sales Results:
Over 18,000 downloads of the free book
321 sales of other two books at regular price
66,026 pages read, which I got paid for because I'm in the KENP program.

Royalty Results
321 sales= estimated royalty--$225.00
66,000 pages read=est. royalty-$380.00 (see why you need to be in this program?)
$605.00 income, less $70 for the ad, left me with a profit of $535.00.
These are the figures for the week of the promotion. Sales continued during the next two weeks, so I earned even more. This promotion also raised my book in rank on Amazon.

I've done Kindle Countdown promotions where I've offered a book for 99 cents and promoted it on numerous websites, FB groups, and Twitter. It takes hours of work, and my profit was minimal. I ran a five-day ad, and the total cost was $130 (from advertising on 20+ sites) and only generated a royalty income of $145.00. Too much work. I won't do that again.

However, if you try any of the sites for promotion (which I have listed under promotion sites) be sure and subscribe to each one you advertise with. That way you'll get the ad, showing your book, in your email inbox. If you don't subscribe, then you'll have no way of knowing if the ad ran or not because they promote through emails, not their website.

BookBub has great information on their blog. I recommend you subscribe to it. Here's one article.

The Top Guides to Online Advertising for Marketing Books.
https://insights.bookbub.com/top-guides-to-online-advertising-for-marketing-books/

Also, take the time to fill out an author profile page on BookBub.
https://www.partners.bookbub.com/authors

If you offer your book for a free promotion and wish to list it on sites that send out emails advertising free books, there are sites providing that service. For a $5 donation, the site below will submit your free promotion to 41 different sites for you. A real time saver!

http://www.submityourbooks.com/free/

Best marketing you can do

Put chapter samples/excerpts in the back of all your books with a link. If Kindle users like the book they're reading, they may just click and buy the next book right then. I didn't do this when I first published, so I pulled my books and reformatted to add those samples. This kind of advertising works for you every day!

IT NEVER ENDS

Marketing is something you'll have to do if you intend to sell books. With more than 40,000 books published each month, it takes work to find readers, because it takes work for readers to find you!

Run Free promotions if you have a series or companion books
Run price promotions
Continue to query bloggers for reviews
Work social media each week/day
Join groups on social media

PAY IT FORWARD

Take opportunities to promote other author's work. You can recommend books on Goodreads, mention interesting articles or blogs on YOUR blog or social media. It's a tough world, so we need to support each other.

ONE LAST THING

Any time you list a link to one of your books, strip it down to the URL. Always make sure it stops after the ASIN number.

Here's what I got when I went to Amazon and clicked on one of my books and then copied the link from the search bar.
http://www.amazon.com/gp/product/B00N0VUNGC/ref=s9_simh_gw_g351_i6_r?pf_rd_m=ATVPDKIKX0DER&pf_rd_s=desktop-2&pf_rd_r=1D0K38CV1RK5DAK45QRV&pf_rd_t=36701&pf_rd_p=2091268722&pf_rd_i=desktop

NEVER use one of those links because all that extra stuff serves as identification markers which is how Amazon determines you sent that URL to the person who clicked it, and they might remove any reviews coming from that link.

A proper URL for your book should stop after the ASIN number and look like this:
http://www.amazon.com/dp/B00NOVUNGC

Below is a good article explaining it.
http://www.sellerlabs.com/blog/super-urls-exposed

Here are books I find helpful and recommend.

Story and Style, by Caryl and Ron McAdoo
This book explains the rules of writing in a way beginners through experienced writers can understand.

Slang and Euphemism Dictionary by Richard A. Spears
A dictionary of oaths, curses, insults, sexual slang, drug talk, college lingo, and related matters.

The Emotion Thesaurus by Angela Ackerman and Becca Puglisi
Great resource with ways to write expressions for every emotion.

Strong Verbs Strong Voice by Ann Everett
Includes simple word lists of stronger verbs to replace weak ones.

Body Language by Ann Everett
List character actions and descriptions for each body part.

REMEMBER

When marketing, you should focus on sustained sales, because they are much more important than those quick spikes you get from Kindle Countdown Deals and Free offers. It's continued sales that keep your book up in ranking.

So, what does that mean? It means doing a Countdown Deal or Free Offer from time to time isn't enough. You must use every avenue available to promote your book/books.

ALL ABOUT ANN

Award winning and Amazon Best-Selling author, Ann Everett embraces her small town upbringing and thinks Texans are some of the funniest people on earth. When speaking at conferences and to writing groups, businesses, book clubs, and non-profit organizations, she incorporates her unique brand of wit, making her programs on marketing, self-publishing, and the benefits of laughter, informative and fun.

Her short stories have appeared in The Green Silk Journal, Snag Today, and Story Teller Magazine.

A member of Northeast Texas Writers' Organization, top reviewer on thenextbigwriter.com, and regular speaker at WordWyse Workshops, she lives on a small lake in Northeast Texas, where she writes, bakes, and fights her addiction to Diet Dr. Pepper.

She's been featured on:
Proud of East Texas with Joan Hallmark, KLTV-TV, Tyler, Texas
East Texas Live and Mid-day, KETK-TV, Tyler, Texas
KTSS-TV, Hope, Arkansas
The Authors Show with Don McCauley, Internet radio show
The Chandler & Brownsboro Statesman, Chandler, Texas
The Daily Tribune, Mt. Pleasant, Texas
Tyler Morning Telegraph, Tyler, Texas

InMagazine, East Texas

Ten things you won't know about Ann by reading her bio:

She's married to her high school sweetheart.
She loves shopping at thrift stores.
She doesn't remember her first kiss.
She hates talking on the telephone.
A really sharp pencil makes her happy.
She secretly wants to get a tattoo.
A charter member of National Honor Society in high school remains one of her biggest surprises.
She's thankful wrinkles aren't painful.
She sucks at math.

ANN'S BOOKS

TELL ME A SECRET

http://www.amazon.com/dp/B00N0VUNGC

TWO WRONGS MAKE A RIGHT

http://www.amazon.com/dp/B00V5M007A

SAY YOU'LL NEVER LOVE ME

http://www.amazon.com/dp/B01BT4A8GQ

LAID OUT AND CANDLE LIT

http://www.amazon.com/dp/B00MYGGW1Y

YOU'RE BUSTING MY NUPTIALS

http://www.amazon.com/dp/B00N06XZPS

TIED WITH A BOW AND NO PLACE TO GO

http://www.amazon.com/dp/B00MYG811I

TIZZY/RIDGE SERIES (Box Set)

http://www.amazon.com/dp/B01ENFPVO2

STRONG VERBS STRONG VOICE

http://www.amazon.com/dp/B00MYG7Y3O

BODY LANGUAGE

http://www.amazon.com/dp/B00XSB3LM2

SWEET THANGS: Southern Recipes from Two Sassy Sisters

http://www.amazon.com/dp/B015NGU8P2

https://store.kobobooks.com/en-us/ebook/sweet-thangs-southern-sweets-from-two-sassy-sisters

Ann's latest book, *Chirp*, a New Adult Romance, has just been named a Kindle Scout Winner.
https://www.amazon.com/dp/B01MT7DXF4

STALK ANN

Facebook
https://www.facebook.com/AuthorAnnEverett/

Website
http://www.anneverett.com

Newsletter
http://www.anneverett.com/join-my-email-list/

Twitter
http://www.twitter.com/TalkinTwang

Pinterest
http://www.pinterest.com/loacl/

Amazon author page
http://www.amazon.com/author/ann.everett

Goodreads profile
https://www.goodreads.com/author/show/5195211.Ann
_Everett

Bookbub profile
https://www.bookbub.com/authors/ann-everett

If you have a desire to join my Street Team, *Sweet Thangs*, or have a comment or question, please contact me through my website contact form. I love hearing from fans.

www.ingramcontent.com/pod-product-compliance
Lightning Source LLC
Chambersburg PA
CBHW070805280326
41934CB00012B/3069